Corporate Culture and Performance

CORPORATE CULTURE AND PERFORMANCE

John P. Kotter

James L. Heskett

THE FREE PRESS

New York London Toronto Sydney Tokyo Singapore

The Free Press
A Division of Simon & Schuster Inc.
1230 Avenue of the Americas
New York, N.Y. 10020

Printed in the United States of America

printing number

5 6 7 8 9 10

Library of Congress Cataloging-in-Publication Data

Kotter, John P.
    Corporate culture and performance/John P. Kotter, James L.
Heskett.
        p. cm.
    Includes bibliographical references and index.
    ISBN 0-02-918467-3
    1. Corporate culture. 2. Organizational effectiveness.
3. Performance. I. Heskett, James L. II. Title.
HD58.7.K68 1992
658—dc20   91–42893
                                                    CIP

CONTENTS

IV. SUMMARY AND CONCLUSIONS

PREFACE

This book's roots go in two different directions. On Kotter's side, there is twenty years of research on managerial behavior, work that has focused recently on the topic of leadership[1] and has twice encountered, but not explored in any depth, the subject of organizational culture.[2] On Heskett's side, there is an even longer history of researching a variety of managerial issues, and more recently, leadership of an effort to create a required course in management for MBAs at Harvard.[3]

Our collaboration began in the summer of 1987. Over a four-year period, we conducted four studies, the ultimate purpose of which was to determine whether there is a relationship between corporate culture and long-term economic performance and, if there is, to clarify the nature of that relationship, to explore why it exists, and to determine whether it can be exploited to augment corporate performance.

The studies were all supported financially by the Division of Research at the Harvard Business School. In addition, nearly forty corporations helped with data collection, and a number of individuals critiqued early drafts of this manuscript. The latter include Louis Barnes, Michael Beer, Richard Boyatzis, Jay Conger, Terry Deal, Nancy Dearman, Daniel Denison, Robert Eccles, Russell Eisenstat, John Gabarro, Linda Hill, Todd Jick, Julie Johnson, Ralph Kilmann, Robert Lambrix, Paul Lawrence, Jay Lorsch, Mal Salter, Edgar Schein, Leonard Schlesinger, David Thomas, Warren Wilhelm, and Michael Winston. This assistance, along with the manuscript-processing skills of Rosemary Brigham and Carolyn Saltiel and the research assistance of James Leahey, Andrew Segal, and Nancy Rothbard, made this book possible.

John P. Kotter
James L. Heskett

I

Introduction

1

THE POWER OF CULTURE

We encounter organizational cultures all the time. When they are not our own, their most visible and unusual qualities seem striking: the look of the traditionally dressed IBM salesman, the commitment to firm and product expressed by employees at Honda or Matsushita, the informality of Apple and many other high-tech companies. When the cultures are our own, they often go unnoticed—until we try to implement a new strategy or program which is incompatible with their central norms and values. Then we observe, first hand, the power of culture.

* * *

The term "culture" originally comes from social anthropology.[1] Late nineteenth- and early twentieth-century studies of "primitive" societies—Eskimo, South Sea, African, Native American—revealed ways of life that were not only different from the more technologically advanced parts of America and Europe but were often very different among themselves.[2] The concept of culture was thus coined to represent, in a very broad and holistic sense, the qualities of any specific human group that are passed from one generation to the next. The *American Heritage Dictionary* defines "culture," more formally, as "the totality of socially transmitted behavior patterns, arts, beliefs, institutions, and all other products of human work and thought characteristics of a community or population."

We have found it helpful to think of *organizational* culture as having two levels, which differ in terms of their visibility and their resistance to change.[3] At the deeper and less visible level, culture refers to values that are shared by the people in a group and that tend to persist over time even when group membership changes. These notions about what is important in life can vary greatly in different companies; in some settings people care deeply about money, in others about technological innovation or employee well-being. At this level culture can be extremely difficult to change, in part because group members are often unaware of many of the values that bind them together.

At the more visible level, culture represents the behavior patterns or style of an organization that new employees are automatically encouraged to follow by their fellow employees. We say, for example, that people in one group have for years been "hard workers," those in another are "very friendly" to strangers, and those in a third always wear very conservative clothes. Culture, in this sense, is still tough to change, but not nearly as difficult as at the level of basic values.

Each level of culture has a natural tendency to influence the other. This is perhaps most obvious in terms of shared values influencing a group's behavior—a commitment to customers, for example, influencing how quickly individuals tend to respond to customer complaints. But causality can flow in the other direction too—behavior and practices can influence values. When employees who have never had any contact with the marketplace begin to interact with customers and their problems and needs, they often begin to value the interests of customers more highly (see exhibit 1.1).

Conceptualized in this way, culture in a business enterprise is not the same as a firm's "strategy" or "structure," although these terms (and others such as "vision" or "mission") are sometimes used almost interchangeably because they can all play an important part, along with the competitive and regulatory environment, in shaping people's behavior (see exhibit 1.2). Strategy is simply a logic for how to achieve movement in some

EXHIBIT 1.1

CULTURE IN AN ORGANIZATION

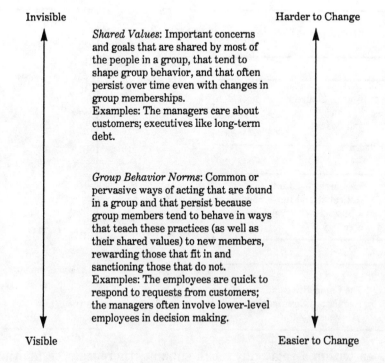

Invisible   Harder to Change

Shared Values: Important concerns and goals that are shared by most of the people in a group, that tend to shape group behavior, and that often persist over time even with changes in group memberships.
Examples: The managers care about customers; executives like long-term debt.

Group Behavior Norms: Common or pervasive ways of acting that are found in a group and that persist because group members tend to behave in ways that teach these practices (as well as their shared values) to new members, rewarding those that fit in and sanctioning those that do not.
Examples: The employees are quick to respond to requests from customers; the managers often involve lower-level employees in decision making.

Visible   Easier to Change

direction.[4] The beliefs and practices called for in a strategy may be compatible with a firm's culture or they may not. When they are not, a company usually finds it difficult to implement the strategy successfully. But even when successfully implemented, the behavior patterns that represent a given strategy are not cultural *unless* most group members tend actively to encourage new members to follow those practices.

Structure refers to certain formal organizational arrangements. Such arrangements may call for behavior that is already pervasive in a firm for cultural reasons. They may call for actions that are not in the culture but are in no way incompatible with it. Or they may call for practices that are at odds with the culture. In this last case, we often find that people differentiate the "formal organization" from the "informal organization."[5]

Although we usually talk about organizational culture in the singular, all firms have multiple cultures—usually associated with different functional groupings or geographic locations.[6]

EXHIBIT 1.2

FOUR FACTORS THAT SHAPE MANAGERIAL BEHAVIOR

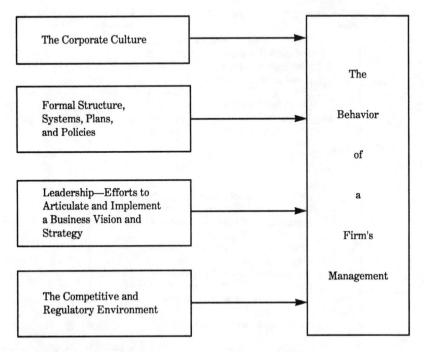

Even within a relatively small subunit, there may be multiple and even conflicting subcultures. Large and geographically dispersed organizations might have hundreds of different cultures. When people talk of "the corporate culture," they usually mean values and practices that are shared across all groups in a firm, at least within senior management. Using the same logic, a "divisional culture" would be the culture that is shared by all the functional and geographical groups in a division of a corporation.

Firms have cultures because the conditions needed for their creation are commonplace. As MIT's Edgar Schein and others have well demonstrated, all that seems to be required is that a group of employees interact over a significant period of time and be relatively successful at whatever they undertake. Solutions that repeatedly appear to solve the problems they encounter tend to become a part of their culture. The longer the solutions seem to work, the more deeply they tend to become embedded in the culture.[7] Thus, if management increases advertising expenditures whenever revenues cease to grow and that action always appears to increase sales significantly, this behavioral pattern will likely become a part of the firm's corporate culture. Depending upon the specific circumstances, a related value or belief—perhaps "Ads are great in a downturn," or "Selective advertising is valuable"—may also become a part of that culture.

Ideas or solutions that become embedded in a culture can originate anywhere: from an individual or a group, at the bottom of the organization or the top. But in firms with strong corporate cultures, these ideas often seem to be associated with a founder or other early leaders[8] who articulate them as a "vision," a "business strategy," a "philosophy," or all three[9] (see exhibit 1.3.).

Once established, organizational cultures often perpetuate themselves in a number of ways. Potential group members may be screened according to how well their values and behavior fit in.[10] Newly selected members may be explicitly taught the group's style.[11] Historical stories or legends may be told again and again to remind everyone of the group's values and what they mean.[12] Managers may explicitly try to act in ways that exemplify the culture and its ideals.[13] Senior members of the group may communicate key values over and over in their daily conversations or through special rituals and ceremonies.[14] People who successfully achieve the ideals inherent in the culture may be recognized and made into heroes.[15] The natural process of identification between younger and older members may encourage the younger members to take on the values and styles of their mentors.[16] Perhaps most fundamental, people who follow cultural norms will be rewarded but those who do not will be penalized.[17]

Cultures can be very stable over time, but they are never static. Crises sometimes force a group to reevaluate some values or set of practices.[18] New challenges can lead to the creation of new ways of doing things. Turnover of key members, rapid assimilation of new employees, diversification into very different businesses, and geographical expansion can all weaken or change a culture.[19]

Sufficient crises and turnover, coupled with the lack of perpetuating mechanisms, can destroy a culture or make it very weak. But conversely, cultures can grow to be extremely strong—where there are many common values, behavior patterns, and practices, and where the levels of culture are tightly interconnected. Continuity of leadership, stable group member-

EXHIBIT 1.3

ONE COMMON PATTERN IN THE EMERGENCE OF CORPORATE CULTURES

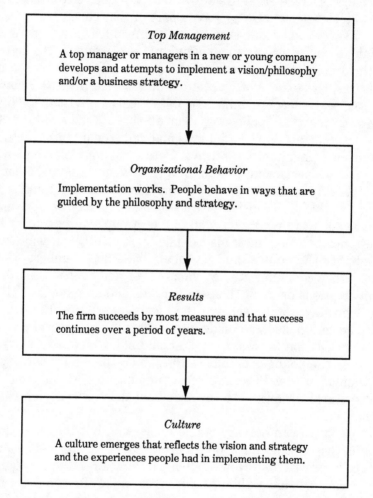

Top Management

A top manager or managers in a new or young company develops and attempts to implement a vision/philosophy and/or a business strategy.

Organizational Behavior

Implementation works. People behave in ways that are guided by the philosophy and strategy.

Results

The firm succeeds by most measures and that success continues over a period of years.

Culture

A culture emerges that reflects the vision and strategy and the experiences people had in implementing them.

ship, geographical concentration, small group size, and considerable success all contribute to the emergence of strong cultures.[20]

Cultures can have powerful consequences, especially when they are strong. They can enable a group to take rapid and coordinated action against a competitor or for a customer. They can also lead intelligent people to walk, in concert, off a cliff.

*   *   *

One of the very earliest examples of modern business research concluded that work groups in organizations could develop their own unique cultures and that those cultures could hurt or help a firm's performance.[21] This idea received limited attention outside academia until the late 1970s[22] when an interrelated group of people, most of them associated with a small set of universities and consulting firms (Harvard, Stanford, MIT, McKinsey, and MAC),[23] began asserting the importance of what they called "corporate" or "organizational" culture. Their claims were based mostly on three kinds of research: of Japanese firms that consistently outperformed their American competition;[24] of U.S. firms that were doing well despite the increasingly competitive business environment that began to emerge in the 1970s;[25] and of companies that were trying to develop and implement competitive strategies to cope with that new environment, but were having difficulty doing so.[26]

In each of these cases, despite differences in initial research focus, terminology, and methodology, the fundamental conclusions were very similar and very dramatic: all firms have corporate cultures, although some have much "stronger" cultures than others; these cultures can exert a powerful effect on individuals and on performance, especially in a competitive environment; this influence may even be greater than all those factors that have been discussed most often in the organizational and business literature—strategy, organizational structure, management systems, financial analysis tools, leadership, etc.; the very best American and Japanese executives often devote time and energy expressly to creating, shaping, or maintaining strong corporate cultures.

The first book-length reports of this work received a great deal of attention. After a decade of increasing competitive intensity in most U.S. industries, an environment in which firms did not perform as well as they did in the 1950s and 1960s, many people were looking for new answers and new ideas, and something in these books rang true. Despite somewhat radical, or at least unconventional, conclusions, the four books published in 1981 and 1982—Ouchi's *Theory Z*, Pascale and Athos's *The Art of Japanese Management*, Deal and Kennedy's *Corporate Cultures*, and Peters and Waterman's *In Search of Excellence*—all became best sellers. *In Search of Excellence* broke nonfiction book sales records.

The resulting impact on both management[27] and public opinion was unusually large. In 1989, less than a decade after the term "corporate culture" came into general use, Time, Inc., blocked a hostile bid by Paramount by arguing that its culture would be destroyed or changed by the takeover, to the detriment of its customers, its shareholders, and society. When the chancery judge ruled in Time's favor, he said (in part) "that there may . . . be instances in which the law might recognize a perceived threat to a 'corporate culture' that is shown to be palpable (for lack of a better word), distinctive, and, advantageous."[28]

The successes of the first four "culture" books encouraged dozens of additional studies. Some of these subsequent studies offered theories about the relationship of culture and performance that depart radically from those found in the first four.[29] A few scholars have even questioned whether there is any generalizable relationship between culture and performance.[30] This more recent work was also critical of earlier ideas about cultural change.[31] Some people have even questioned whether a firm's management can successfully manipulate a corporate culture, especially since it is difficult to find convincingly documented cases of cultural change.[32]

It was against this background that we launched our research in 1987.

*   *   *

Between August 1987 and January 1991, we conducted four studies to determine whether a relationship exists between corporate culture and long-term economic performance, to clarify the nature of and the reasons for such a relationship, and to discover whether and how that relationship can be exploited to enhance a firm's performance.

Many factors influence the performance of firms. Here, we are interested in the potential impact of one element only—corporate culture (*not* subunit cultures). Because of the complexity of the relationships involved and the difficulty of measuring various factors, research of this sort is almost impossible to do with great rigor. Nevertheless, we tried in our four studies to be as systematic and precise as possible.[33]

Our first inquiry was focused on the largest 9 or 10 firms in twenty-two different U.S. industries. We attempted to test the most widely accepted theory linking corporate culture to long-term economic performance. The results of this work are reported in Chapter 2. In the second study, we tested two more culture/performance theories, this time by examining in more depth a small subset (22) of the original 207 firms. This work is discussed in Chapters 3 and 4; Chapter 5 is a detailed description of one of those cases. The third study examined 20 firms that appear to have had cultures that hurt their economic performance. The results of that inquiry can be found in Chapter 6. Our last project focused on 10 firms that seem to have changed their corporate cultures within the recent past and then benefitted economically. That study is discussed in Chapters 7 and 8; Chapters 9 and 10 are descriptions of two of those ten cases.

In total, our studies strongly suggest that the early corporate culture books were very much on the right track, although they failed in some important ways—not unusual in the case of pioneering work. More specifically, our studies show that:

1. *Corporate culture can have a significant impact on a firm's long-term economic performance.* We found that firms with cultures that emphasized all the key managerial constituencies (customers, stockholders, and employees) and leadership from managers at all levels outperformed firms that did not have those cultural traits by a huge margin. Over an eleven-year period, the former increased revenues by an average of 682 percent versus 166 percent for the latter, expanded their work forces by 282 percent versus 36 percent, grew their stock prices by 901 percent versus 74 percent, and improved their net incomes by 756 percent versus 1 percent.

2. *Corporate culture will probably be an even more important factor in determining the success or failure of firms in the next decade.* Performance-degrading cultures have a negative financial impact for a number of reasons, the most significant being their tendency to inhibit firms from adopting needed strategic or tactical changes. In a world that is changing at an increasing rate, one would predict that unadaptive cultures will have an even larger negative financial impact in the coming decade.

3. *Corporate cultures that inhibit strong long-term financial performance are not rare; they develop easily, even in firms that are full of reasonable and intelligent people.* Cultures

that encourage inappropriate behavior and inhibit change to more appropriate strategies tend to emerge slowly and quietly over a period of years, usually when firms are performing well. Once these cultures exist, they can be enormously difficult to change because they are often invisible to the people involved, because they help support the existing power structure in the firm, and for many other reasons.

4. *Although tough to change, corporate cultures can be made more performance enhancing.* Such change is complex, takes time, and requires leadership, which is something quite different from even excellent management. That leadership must be guided by a realistic vision of what kinds of cultures enhance performance—a vision that is currently hard to find in either the business community or the literature on culture.

What kinds of corporate cultures enhance long term economic performance? We address this basic issue next.

II

The Performance Question:

WHAT KIND OF CORPORATE CULTURES ENHANCE LONG-TERM ECONOMIC PERFORMANCE?

2

STRONG CULTURES

Almost all books on corporate culture state or imply a relationship to long-term economic performance. Although these theories are rarely very explicit and vary endlessly, they basically fall into three categories.

The most elegant of the culture/performance perspectives, and the one most widely reported, associates "strong" cultures with excellent performance.[1] In a strong corporate culture, almost all managers share a set of relatively consistent values and methods of doing business. New employees adopt these values very quickly. In such a culture, a new executive is just as likely to be corrected by his subordinates as by his bosses if he violates the organization's norms. Firms with strong cultures are usually seen by outsiders as having a certain "style"—the Procter & Gamble or Johnson & Johnson "way of doing things." They often make some of their shared values known in a creed or mission statement and seriously encourage all their managers to follow that statement. Furthermore, the style and values of a strong culture tend not to change much when a new CEO takes charge—their roots go deep.

The logic of how cultural strength relates to performance involves three ideas, the first of which is goal alignment. In a firm with a strong culture, employees tend to march to the same drummer. That is no small achievement in a world full of specialization and other forms of diversity. One CEO of a medium-sized organization recently expressed this idea in the following way: "I cannot imagine trying to run a business today with a weak or nonexistent culture; why, people would be going off in a hundred different directions."

Strong cultures are also often said to help business performance because they create an unusual level of motivation in employees. Sometimes the assertion is made that shared values and behaviors make people feel good about working for a firm; that feeling of commitment or loyalty then is said to make people strive harder. Sometimes certain practices believed to be common among firms with strong cultures are said to make work intrinsically rewarding. Involving people in decision making and recognizing their contributions would be two common examples.

Occasionally, strong cultures are also said to help performance because they provide needed structure and controls without having to rely on a stifling formal bureaucracy that can dampen motivation and innovation.

Terry Deal and Allan Kennedy point to Tandem Computers as a typical example of a strong-culture company.[2] It was "founded on a well-ordered set of management beliefs and practices." The firm is said to have "no formal organization chart and few formal rules," yet employees keep "off each others toes" and work productively "in the same direction" because of the "unwritten rules and shared understandings." This culture is maintained because top management spends considerable time "in training and in communicating the management philosophy and the essence of the company," because achievements consistent with the culture "are regularly recognized on bulletin boards as Our Latest Greatests," and because rituals such as the Friday afternoon "beer-bust" symbolize that culture. All this makes employees feel like they belong to an exclusive club. Most develop great respect for and loyalty to that club, a feeling which often translates into long hours of hard, productive work.[3]

Although in a very different industry, Northwestern Mutual is said to have a corporate culture as strong as Tandem's. Each summer, this Milwaukee-based life insurance company hosts a three-day convention for its agents and home office staff, the centerpiece of which is an elaborate (almost Broadway-like) show starring the CEO and other executives. That show always includes an entertaining skit that emphasizes, in a not very subtle manner, the firm's core values. It also includes a lot of recognition of individuals who have succeeded in upholding those values.

The most famous strong-culture company is probably IBM. As far back as the mid-1930s, IBM employees had the reputation of being loyal and highly motivated. There was a surprising amount of consensus concerning how to conduct business. That philosophy valued, above all, (1) respect for the dignity and the rights of each person in the firm, (2) giving the best customer service of any company in the world, and (3) pursuing all tasks with the objective of accomplishing them in a superior way. Tom Watson, Sr., is said to be the individual most responsible for this culture. In 1962, his son and successor as chairman of IBM, Tom Watson, Jr., made the case for the strong-culture perspective in a speech at Columbia University. Said Watson, Jr.: "The basic philosophy, spirit, and desire of an organization have far more to do with its relative achievements than do technological or economic resources, organizational structure, innovation, and timing. All these things weigh heavily on success. But they are, I think, transcended by how strongly the people in the organization believe in its basic precepts and how faithfully they carry them out."[4]

This viewpoint appears to be widely accepted in certain quarters.[5] We have interviewed dozens of executives who seem genuinely to believe it, some because of a casual reading of the books on corporate culture published in the 1980s—especially Pascale and Athos's *The Art of Japanese Management* and Deal and Kennedy's *Corporate Cultures*.[6] Others appear to accept this idea because it is relatively easy to find specific cases in the business press that seem to confirm the theory—for example, Wal-Mart, where a strong culture that emphasizes, among other things, the founder's frugality, hard work, and dedication to customers has apparently produced spectacular results. The theory is even popular with some scholars. One 1988 business doctoral dissertation goes so far to say that "since the current literature already provides enough support to the assumption that strong cultures lead to higher performance, this study goes beyond that."[7]

This perspective is important for at least three reasons: (1) it was probably the first major attempt to link corporate culture and long-term economic performance; (2) it highlights the effect of a strong culture on goal alignment, motivation, and control; and (3) it captured the attention of a lot of people.

But despite its popularity, questions have been raised about this theory. One has to do with causality. This perspective says that strong cultures cause strong performance, yet the reverse is known to occur too—strong performance can help to create strong cultures.[8] Could the latter explain most or all of any relationship found between culture strength and performance?

Another question concerns where the "cultural drummer" is directing people.[9] If the direction is good, then a strong culture might logically help a firm do well. But what if it is bad? What if people all run, hand in hand, in the wrong direction?[10] Even Pascale and Athos point out that under these circumstances, you can end up with a situation that resembles the Third Reich.[11] Peters and Waterman put it this way: "The brainwashed members of an extremist political sect are no more conformist in their central beliefs" than are people in some of their "excellent" companies![12]

Proponents of this theory sometimes acknowledge the second issue, but counter that strong cultures very rarely go berserk. They seem to feel that the benefits of a strong culture simply outweigh the risks, especially in an increasingly competitive world where excellent performance does not come easily. Besides, they seem to ask, what is the alternative? A stifling bureaucracy is clearly not a better way to keep activities under control. Only exceptionally strong leaders seem able to create the kind of alignment and motivation characteristic of a strong culture.[13] Yet with powerful leaders there are even more risks. Not only might a leader send a firm in the wrong direction, he or she might retire without leaving any successors. The power vacuum that would result could be disastrous.

*   *   *

Testing a set of ideas like those underlying the strong-culture perspective is difficult because the main concepts are hard to measure and collecting relevant data is rarely a simple task. As a result, our own efforts to check the validity of this first theory are far from perfect in any methodologically absolute sense. Nonetheless, we think the conclusions from that work are both interesting and revealing.

Our approach was the following. First, we picked 207 firms from twenty-two different U.S. industries.[14] Our only objective in this particular selection was to get a large and diverse sample of companies. The industries included aerospace, airlines, apparel/textiles, automotive, banking, beverages, chemicals, computers and office equipment, food/packaged goods, forest products/paper, life insurance, personal care, petroleum refining and marketing, pharmaceutical/drugs, publishing/printing, retailing/food and drugs, retailing/non-food and drugs, rubber, savings and loan, telecommunications, and textiles. The firms included well known names like Dow Chemical, Coca-Cola, and Ford along with relatively unknown companies like Paccar, Kellwood, Calfed, and Manhattan. (See exhibit A.1 in the appendix for a complete listing of these firms.)

Using a questionnaire survey (described in exhibit A.2), we constructed "culture strength" indices for almost all of these firms (a complete list of these indices is given in exhibit A.4. A small sampling is shown in exhibit 2.1).

We then calculated measures of economic performance for as many companies as possible for the period 1977–1988.[15] Three different methods were used since no single index seemed to fully capture the concept of economic performance: (1) average yearly increase in net income (see exhibit A.5), (2) average yearly return on investment (see exhibit A.6), and (3) average yearly increase in stock price (see exhibit A.7). The first of these measures is probably the least valid because it is most vulnerable to accounting manipulations and can be distorted by merger and acquisition activity. Nevertheless, we included it since managers still look to net income growth as a basic index of economic performance. The second measure—average yearly return on investment—is less subject to such distortion. The third index, based on average yearly increase in stock price, has the virtue of being an external measure.

Finally, we examined the relationship between the performance and culture strength indices. We did the same with a second set of numbers created by adjusting the original indices

EXHIBIT 2.1

A SAMPLING OF THE STRENGTH-OF-CULTURE INDICES
CREATED FOR OUR FIRST STUDY

---

1 = Very Strong Corporate Culture circa 1976–1986

5 = Very Weak Corporate Culture circa 1976–1986

Procter & Gamble	1.18
IBM	1.34
Time Inc.	1.91
Quaker Oats	2.21
Mobil	2.52
Gillette	2.64
New York Life	2.81
Monsanto	2.92
Chase Manhattan	3.09
Baxter Travenol	3.30
Federated Department Stores	3.56
USX	3.77
Pitney Bowes	3.93
Eastern (Airlines)	4.30

The construction of these indices is explained in exhibit A.2 in the Appendix.

to show relative culture strength and relative performance within industries. In each case, the results were almost identical.

Exhibit 2.2 shows culture strength vs. market value growth numbers (unadjusted) plotted on a graph. This diagram is worth studying for a moment. (The two other performance measures are shown in exhibit A.8.) Exhibit 2.2 seems to show a random scattering of dots, but it does not. There is a positive correlation

EXHIBIT 2.2

CULTURE STRENGTH AND MARKET VALUE GROWTH*

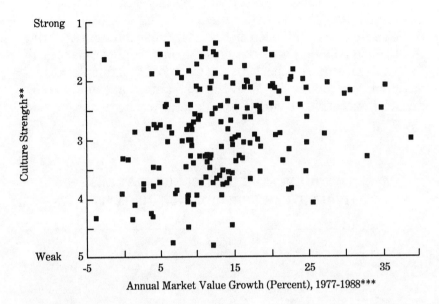

* Nine firms had returns either above 40 percent or below −5 percent and are not shown.
** See exhibits A.3 and A.4.
*** See exhibit A.7.

between corporate culture and long-term economic performance, but, as the diagram clearly shows, not a very strong one.[16] It seems a firm can have a strong culture and poor performance or a weak culture and excellent performance. Neither possibility can be explained by the strong-culture perspectives.

Within the limits of this methodology, we conclude from this study that there is a positive relationship between strength of corporate culture and long-term economic performance, but it is a modest relationship. The statement "Strong cultures create excellent performance" appears to be just plain wrong.

*   *   *

To understand the limitations of this perspective, we found it useful to examine those firms that received strong cultural strength scores yet weak performance scores—that is, firms whose experiences seem to have most clearly violated this theory. The companies in our study that fit that description are H.F. Ahmanson,

Citicorp, Coors, General Motors, Goodyear, K Mart, Kroger, J.C. Penney, Procter & Gamble, and Sears (see exhibit 2.3).

These firms share two relevant characteristics. First, they are relatively well known for having strong cultures. Second, these cultures have all been criticized by some observers during the 1980s for having hurt the firms' economic performances.

General Motors is perhaps the most visible example. Critics have pointed an accusing finger at its habit of allowing narrow financial executives to make key design, production, and mar-

EXHIBIT 2.3

FIRMS WITH RELATIVELY STRONG CULTURES AND RELATIVELY WEAK PERFORMANCE CIRCA 1977–1988

	Corporate Culture Score	Index of Performance Based on Annual Net Income Growth*	Average Annual Return on Capital (%)	Average Annual Growth of Stock Price (%)
	1 = Strong 5 = Very Weak	Strong** Performance = 27–170	Strong** Performance = 13–40	Strong** Performance = 17–47
H.F. Ahmanson	1.68	12.4	4.49	12.80
Citicorp	1.52	18.2	4.98	10.30
Coors	1.67	9.2	7.69	4.20
General Motors	1.80	9.2	10.59	3.27
Goodyear	1.75	17.0	6.72	8.21
K Mart	1.86	15.6	9.19	8.72
Kroger	2.21	22.0	8.10	6.09
J.C. Penney	1.95	16.0	8.90	10.65
Procter & Gamble	1.18	16.4	13.00	6.42
Sears	2.23	14.8	7.19	5.87

* See exhibit A.5 for an explanation of the measure.
** Strong Performance = top quartile of all scores.

keting decisions. They have argued that its propensity toward adversarial labor relations has cost the firm a lot of money. They have said that the value GM managers have placed on economies of scale has led the company to ignore other important factors. And they have pointed out that executive behavior based on the assumption that the world is a relatively stable and predictable place is simply out of touch with reality.[17]

Similar criticism has been leveled at Sears. Its traditions have allegedly allowed "decentralization" to mean autonomous fiefdoms inside the firm, fiefdoms that have resisted needed change. Managers in the firm have been described as having a propensity to focus inward, sometimes ignoring competition and shifts in consumer preferences. These and other aspects of the Sears culture have been reported to have hurt its performance greatly over the past two or three decades.[18]

Likewise, the conservative and nepotistic aspects of Coors's corporate culture were a central reason why *Financial World* magazine included the firm in its 1987 survey, "The 10 Worst-Managed Companies in America."[19] The centralized and bureaucratic behavior in Goodyear's culture has been identified by its own new CEO as a major reason why that company's performance has been disappointing.[20] The highly analytical, methodical, and risk-averse behavior in Procter & Gamble's culture has been criticized both by outsiders and by some of its own management.[21] K Mart's lack of a strong customer service ethos has been said to be its major weakness in its competition with Wal-Mart.[22] The arrogance in Citicorp's culture has been cited for leading the firm into bad business deals and alienating some of its customers.[23]

These cases suggest that one criticism of the strong-culture theory—that the cultural drummer can lead a firm into decline as well as into success—may be valid. Apparently, strong cultures can include dysfunctional elements as well as vigorous, functional ones. Strong cultures can lead people—even reasonable, thoughtful people—astray. Extreme cases of this may be very rare, but the information in exhibit 2.3 suggests that mild examples of this phenomena are not at all unusual.

How can this happen? The list of firms in exhibit 2.3 may have the answer. All these companies have, for the most part, done unusually well sometime in the past. Citicorp is typical. At the turn of the century it went from being the twelfth-largest commercial bank in New York to the largest and strongest bank in the country. Although it suffered during the Depression, as did practically all banks, its assets grew nearly fivefold from 1949 to 1970. During that period its profits increased 700 percent.[24] Sears was so phenomenally successful that by the early 1960s it was more than five times larger than any of its competitors. Coors grew from being the fourteenth-largest U.S. brewer in 1959 to the fourth-largest in just fourteen years. General Motors was so successful that it became the largest corporation in the world. Goodyear beat all its rivals to become the world's largest tire and rubber firm. K Mart increased its net income over 600 percent in the decade 1968–1978. Kroger outdistanced massive supermarket competition. H.F. Ahmanson grew to be the largest firm in the savings and loan industry. Procter & Gamble became the premier packaged-goods company in America.

In Chapter 6, we will have more to say about the association between success and cultures that can undermine future performance. For now, one observation will do. As critics of the strong-culture perspective have said, although the theory posits that a strong culture creates good performance, causality goes the other way too; good long-term performance can cause or reinforce a strong culture. But with much success, that strong culture can easily become somewhat arrogant, inwardly focused, politicized, and bureaucratic. In an increasingly competitive and rapidly changing world, that kind of culture unquestionably undermines economic performance. It can blind top management to the need for new business strategies. It can also make strategic change, even when attempted, difficult or impossible to implement.

*   *   *

Two more questions are raised by this study: Why are some firms with weak cultures able to perform well? And if this theory is wrong, why do so many intelligent individuals accept it?

Exhibit 2.4 lists those firms that are relevant to the first question. Four companies in our original sample of 207 had weak cultures but very good performance: McGraw-Hill, SmithKline, General Cinema, and Pitney Bowes. The weak corporate cultures in all four cases seem to be a result of many and/or large acquisitions made by these firms immediately preceding or during the 1977–1988 period. The strong performances appear related to monopolistic market positions. McGraw-Hill, for

EXHIBIT 2.4

FIRMS WITH WEAK CULTURES AND STRONG ECONOMIC PERFORMANCE CIRCA 1977–1988

Company	Corporate Culture Score	Index of Performance Based on Annual Net Income Growth*	Average Annual Return on Capital (%)	Average Annual Growth of Stock Price (%)
	1 = Strong 5 = Very Weak	Strong ** Performance = 27–170	Strong ** Performance = 13–40	Strong ** Performance = 17–47
McGraw-Hill	3.38	26.4	19.76	18.57
SmithKline	3.59	48.8	24.76	13.46
General Cinema	3.67	37.3	11.98	22.80
Pitney Bowes	3.93	48.2	14.40	25.68

* See exhibit A.5 for an explanation of the measure.
** Strong Performance = top quartile of all scores.

example, bought Standard & Poors in 1966, four TV stations in 1972, Datapro Research Corporation in 1976, DRI in 1979, and a variety of smaller firms in the early 1980s, all of which had cultures that were somewhat different from the company's book/ magazine core and all of which had very strong (and hence, very profitable) market positions. Apparently, the different cultures of the acquired firms were not integrated to form a new corporate culture. Nevertheless, these firms continued to perform well because of their monopolistic market positions and the relative autonomy that the weak corporate culture allowed.

It is possible, of course, that as firms become more diverse over time, through acquisitions and internal diversification, corporate cultures of necessity become weaker; but our findings don't support that idea. When we located measures of business diversity for all our firms and correlated them with our strength of corporate cultures scores, the resulting correlation coefficient was negative but very small.[25] Business diversity appears to explain little of the variation in our strength of corporate culture scores.

Exhibit 2.5 suggests an answer to the question about why so many people believe in the strong-culture theory. People who know these firms, all of whom have high culture strength scores and high long-term performance scores, often use the logic of this perspective to help explain why these companies have done well. They say that the unusual sense of direction shared by

EXHIBIT 2.5

FIRMS WITH STRONG CULTURES AND STRONG LONG-TERM ECONOMIC PERFORMANCE CIRCA 1977–1988

Company	Corporate Culture Score	Index of Performance Based on Annual Net Income Growth*	Average Annual Return on Capital (%)	Average Annual Growth of Stock Price (%)
	1 = Strong 5 = Very Weak	Strong ** Performance = 27–170	Strong ** Performance = 13–40	Strong ** Performance = 17–47
Albertsons	1.86	34.1	12.64	27.82
Anheuser-Busch	1.63	43.7	12.43	23.30
ConAgra	1.91	103.1	13.34	35.65
Cooper Tire	2.00	43.0	10.83	30.88
Digital	1.93	50.2	12.96	20.65
Dow Jones	1.83	33.6	26.64	17.07
Gannett	1.91	34.0	16.04	16.65
Hewlett-Packard	1.93	40.2	16.35	17.50
New York Times	1.76	36.5	14.51	22.98
Rubbermaid	1.80	35.7	16.97	22.90
VF	1.79	39.8	19.05	24.57
Wal-Mart	1.12	139.0	18.70	46.67

* See exhibit A.5 for an explanation of the measure.
** Strong Performance = top quartile of all scores.

managers at ConAgra has most assuredly helped long-term re-sults. They say that the level of motivation at Wal-Mart, a prod-uct of its top leadership and its culture, has certainly boosted the firm's performance. They say, in other words, that this strong-culture theory seems to work well—at least for these firms.

And in a sense it does. The problem with this perspective (which we shall call Theory I) is not that its main ideas are wrong. On the contrary, the notion of the potential power of an aligned and motivated group is very insightful. Those ideas are relevant to a large number of organizations today and should continue to be very relevant in the foreseeable future. The prob-lem with the strong-culture theory, as we will see, is simply that it is incomplete. In its elegance, it overlooks too much. Much too much.

3

STRATEGICALLY APPROPRIATE CULTURES

A second perspective on the relationship of culture and performance directly addresses a major criticism of the first. Theory II explicitly states the direction that cultures must align and motivate employees if they are to enhance company performance. The key concept employed is that of "fit."

This second perspective asserts that the content of a culture, in terms of which values and behaviors are common, is as important, if not more important, than its strength. Further, it asserts that there is no such thing as generically good cultural content; there is no one-size-fits-all "winning" culture that works well anywhere. Instead, in Theory II, a culture is good only if it "fits" its context, whether one means by context the objective conditions of its industry, that segment of its industry specified by a firm's strategy, or the business strategy itself. According to this perspective, only those contextually or strategically appropriate cultures will be associated with excellent performance. The better the fit, the better the performance; the poorer the fit, the poorer the performance.[1]

Theory II predicts that a culture characterized by rapid decision making and no bureaucratic behavior will enhance performance in the highly competitive deal-making environment of a mergers and acquisitions advisory firm but might hurt performance in a traditional life insurance company. Likewise, a culture in which managers place a very high value on excellent technology might help a computer manufacturer but would be inappropriate for a symphony orchestra. A culture favoring seat-of-the-pants decision making might be fine in a small firm but detrimental in a large one. A culture in which people value stable and tall hierarchical structures might work well in a slow-moving environment but be totally inappropriate in a very fast-moving and competitive industry.

Although this perspective tends to be vague about what precisely constitutes "good fit," the logic here is not unappealing. The notion that a small high-tech firm might need a different culture from that of a large bank has an obvious ring of truth. One study even gives limited empirical credence to the idea.[2]

It is not difficult to find examples that seem consistent with this viewpoint. The case of VF Corporation may be typical. Once known as Vanity Fair, this apparel manufacturer thrived for years in the highly competitive marketplace for commodity clothing—underwear, sports shirts, jeans. It did so with a strategy that called for good basic products at a very low cost. Those familiar with the firm agree that its culture helped enormously. In that culture, managers emphasized discipline and quality, were manufacturing- and engineering-driven, valued conservative financial policies, and were almost obsessive about controlling inventories. Although it is hard to imagine such a culture working well in an advertising firm, or even in a high-fashion apparel company, it fit VF's business environment very well, and the long-term economic payoff was impressive: between 1978 and 1984, for example, net income rose over 400 percent.

A more visible example would be Swissair, an international airline with a culture in which managers have emphasized customer service, on-time performance, good equipment, conservative financing, and a feeling of kinship among employees not unlike that found in the traditionally close Swiss family. In an industry with excess capacity, meeting customers' needs is important to long-term economic performance, and Swissair's culture has helped greatly in this regard. Although that culture differs in a number of respects from that found at VF, it fits well Swissair's strategy to compete in the long-haul international airline service business catering primarily to business travelers. With this culture, Swissair's performance in the turbulent 1980s has been consistently strong.

A successful high-tech start-up company usually has a culture different from that of either VF or Swissair—one characterized by minimal bureaucracy, relatively egalitarian relationships, an environment that loves creativity and talented people, and an unusual degree of straightforwardness in internal communications. Such a culture would probably not help a commodity apparel company or an international airline produce outstanding performance, but it fits well the innovation-based strategies that small technology firms use to win against more established and better financed competition.

Theory II seems consistent with the experiences of many other organizations. It corrects for a major error in the strong-cultures perspective (Theory I). Nevertheless, it also has critics who point out its seemingly static nature. They ask: What happens when the environment of an industry changes?

Research by Gordon Donaldson and Jay Lorsch is unusually revealing on this point.[3] They studied a dozen large and well-known U.S. companies. Among the patterns they report are these: (1) strong founders are particularly important in establishing corporate cultures[4] that are both internally consistent and sensible in light of objective environmental conditions (i.e., that fit their environments); (2) these cultures help managers deal with the need to make an ongoing stream of complex decisions by making the decision process easier, more consistent, and better in light of industry conditions; (3) if the environment doesn't change radically, a firm can go for decades with only minor modifications to its corporate culture; (4) but if an industry does change in some significant way, cultural change is too slow to prevent substantial deterioration of economic performance. In the cases they studied, economic events had to threaten the very existence of the firm before managers would seriously question their culture, and even then a new CEO was needed to slowly build (and with a lot of false starts) a consensus around a new culture.[5] The implication here is that the fit between culture and environment may be associated with short-term economic performance, but no single cultural formula is associated with long-term performance, *especially* in an era in which change seems to be the rule.

There is a segment of the financial community that agrees strongly with this conclusion.[6] Their model of the relationship between culture and performance is diametrically opposed to Theory I. Advocates of that perspective believe in a *negative* correlation between culture strength and long-term economic performance because cultures (they believe) stop firms from adapting asset deployment to fit changing conditions. This is one of the rationales voiced by corporate raiders and their supporters.

Proponents of Theory II acknowledge this criticism, but tend to disagree strongly with the "raiders" perspective. They seem to believe that cultures can be changed from within, perhaps with some difficulty, and that intelligent managers will surely do just that to maintain a strategically appropriate fit between culture and context.

*   *   *

To test this second perspective about the relationship of culture and performance, we selected a group of 22 from our original 207 firms for more in-depth investigation.[7] Those chosen were American Airlines, Albertsons, H.F. Ahmanson, Anheuser-Busch, Archer Daniels Midland, Bankers Trust, Citicorp, Con-Agra, Coors, Dayton Hudson, Fieldcrest Cannon, Golden West, Hewlett-Packard, Northwest Airlines, J.C. Penney, PepsiCo, Shell, Springs, Texaco, Wal-Mart, Winn-Dixie, and Xerox. As exhibit 3.1 shows, these companies came from ten different industries. All had relatively strong cultures, but as Exhibit 3.2 demonstrates, twelve of the firms significantly outperformed the other matched group of ten during the period 1977–1988. (Additional information on these firms can be found in exhibits A.9 and A.10.)

None of the "lower performers" performed badly in an absolute sense; a few did very well. But they clearly did not do as well as the "higher performers" in their industry. On average, the higher performers increased their net incomes three times more than the lower performers. The first group's stock rose between 400 and 500 percent from 1977 to 1988 versus 100 per

EXHIBIT 3.1

THE FIRMS IN THE SECOND STUDY

Industry	Group 1			Group 2		
	FIRM	HEADQUARTERS	1989 REVENUES (IN BILLIONS)	FIRM	HEADQUARTERS	1989 REVENUES (IN BILLIONS)
1. Airlines	American	Dallas	$10.48	Northwest	Minneapolis	$6.55
2. Banking	Bankers Trust	New York	$7.26	Citicorp	New York	$37.97
3. Beverages	Anheuser-Busch	St. Louis	$9.48	Coors	Golden, Col.	$1.76
	PepsiCo	Purchase, N.Y.	$15.24			
4. Computers & Office Equipment	Hewlett-Packard	Santa Clara	$11.90	Xerox	Stamford, Conn.	$16.81
5. Food/Packaged Goods	ConAgra	Omaha	$11.34	Archer Daniels Midland	Decatur, Ill.	$7.93
6. Petroleum	Shell	Houston	$21.81	Texaco	White Plains, N.Y.	$32.42

7. Retail/Food & Drugs	Albertsons	Boise	$7.42	Winn-Dixie	Jacksonville, Fla.	$9.15
8. Retail/Non-Food & Drugs	Dayton Hudson	Minneapolis	$13.64	J.C. Penney	Dallas	$13.41
	Wal-Mart	Bentonville, Ark.	$25.81			
9. Savings & Loan	Golden West	Oakland	$1.9	H.F. Ahmanson	Los Angeles	$4.38
10. Textiles	Springs Industries	Fort Mill, S.C.	$1.91	Fieldcrest Cannon	Eden, N.C.	$1.36

EXHIBIT 3.2

DIFFERENCES IN PERFORMANCE AMONG THE FIRMS IN THE
SECOND STUDY

	Index of Annual Net Income Growth*	Annual Return on Invested Capital (%)	Annual Growth of Stock Price (%)
THE HIGHER PERFORMERS			
American Airlines	23.5	4.69	23.69
Bankers Trust	45.3	9.84	20.43
Anheuser-Busch	43.7	12.43	23.30
PepsiCo	22.2	12.95	14.10
Hewlett-Packard	40.2	16.35	17.50
ConAgra	103.1	13.34	35.65
Shell	20.7	10.13	14.96
Albertsons	34.1	12.64	27.82
Dayton Hudson	32.1	10.09	17.35
Wal-Mart	139.0	18.70	46.67
Golden West	39.2	5.37	24.97
Springs Industries	24.0	7.02	15.53
Mean Scores	47.26	11.13	23.50
THE LOWER PERFORMERS			
Northwest Airlines	10.3	5.24	10.65
Citicorp	18.2	4.98	10.30
Coors	9.2	7.69	4.20
Xerox	13.1	8.86	4.35
Archer Daniels Midland	27.7	9.78	18.58
Texaco	9.9	5.36	4.70
Winn-Dixie	16.4	16.40	5.24
J.C. Penney	16.0	8.90	10.65
H.F. Ahmanson	12.4	4.49	12.80
Fieldcrest Cannon	8.3	5.64	6.40
Mean Scores	14.15	7.73	8.79

* See exhibit A.4 for an explanation of the measure.

cent for the lower performers. The one group averaged a return on invested capital of 11.13 percent; the second had average returns of 7.73 percent.

We gathered publicly available information on the content of the cultures in all twenty-two firms, mostly through articles in the business press. Then, before we visited most of these companies, we interviewed a select group of seventy-five experienced and highly regarded industry analysts,[8] individuals who followed one, two, or, in a few cases, three of these firms. We asked the analysts a number of questions about the culture of those companies in which we were interested and in which they specialized (see exhibit A.11 for a copy of this survey). Information from those interviews allowed us to compare the fit between culture and context in the twelve higher-performing firms with that in the ten lower-performing firms.

To check whether the data we were collecting on cultural content was even relevant, we asked each interviewee whether the cultures actually had any impact on performance at those firms in our sample in which he or she specialized. More specifically, we asked if culture "helped" a company's performance, "hurt" it, "helped and hurt" it, or "had little or no impact" (see exhibit 3.3).

Financial analysts have been stereotyped as people who ignore soft data. With that in mind, the results presented in exhibit 3.3 are interesting indeed. They overwhelmingly felt that culture helped the twelve higher-performing companies. In most cases they also felt that culture hurt the lower performers. This was almost unanimously true for the firms with the lowest absolute performance scores. Incredibly, only one of the seventy-five interviewees said he thought the culture of one firm had little or no impact on its performance.

Because all the firms had cultures of relatively equal strength, the data in Exhibit 3.3 opens the possibility that differences in cultural content may be responsible for the differences in performance, as Theory II asserts. To test that idea, we asked each interviewee "How well has the culture at (one company he or she followed) fit the market, competitive, technological, and other environments in which the firm has found itself" during the late 1970s and early 1980s?

The analysts who followed department stores answered this question as follows. First, they said that the culture/

EXHIBIT 3.3

CORPORATE CULTURE'S IMPACT ON LONG-TERM ECONOMIC
PERFORMANCE*

	The Twelve Higher-Performing Firms	The Ten Lower-Performing Firms
Culture has helped performance	43 responses	5 responses
Culture has hurt performance	1	29
Culture has both helped and hurt performance	6	10
Culture has had little or no impact on performance	1	0
Not sure	3	4

* Based on interviews with industry analysts described in exhibit A.9 in the Appendix.

environment fit at Wal-Mart was much better than at J.C. Penney during the period under observation: 1977–1988. When we asked why they thought this was so, we were told how both firms have roots in small-town America. Sam Walton, the founder of Wal-Mart, actually worked for Penney's for a few years. In their earliest days, both emphasized customer satisfaction, entrepreneurship, and treating employees well. But by the late 1970s, we were told, the cultures and environments of the two firms were distinctly different. Managers at Wal-Mart tried to attract good people and motivate them to work hard, were obsessed with improvement, dedicated themselves to the kind of customer that comes to Wal-Mart for good values, and inspired their employees to behave more like merchants than clerks. Wal-Mart managers also were said to emphasize the founder's frugality, productivity through the intelligent use of technology, and genuine care for employees. By that time, Penney stores, on average, had moved into more competitive urban areas. Yet their culture was reportedly not nearly as competitive. Penney managers still emphasized treating employees well and giving the customer value, although much less than in earlier periods. But they also encouraged large and costly bureaucracies ("You need competent staff groups" say Penney managers) as well as performance standards that some people have called mediocre ("We aren't hard on our people"). They were said to be not very technologically oriented, despite all the new technology being offered to retailers ("You can get carried away with technology and forget retailing"). And they created an exceptionally inbred promotions process ("Promotion from within to motivate people is good") that interviewees felt would not help the firm change very easily.

Similar stories were told about Golden West versus H.F. Ahmanson, Anheuser-Busch versus Coors, and all the rest. In each case, one of the two firms was described as having a corporate culture that better fit its context—especially the competitive situation in its key markets. That is, its values and practices better fit the needs of customers in light of the alternatives offered by competitors, better fit the situation in labor markets, and better fit the conditions in financial markets. In cases where firms had divisions in two or more different businesses (e.g., Xerox and Hewlett-Packard), analysts often pointed out that one of the two firms also had better fits at the level of division culture. And consistently, the firm with the better fit (or fits) was the superior performer. Although such stories obviously do not prove anything, they certainly give weight to the main assertion in this second perspective. See exhibit 3.4.

To further test the ideas in Theory II, we asked interviewees to quantify their answers to the culture/context fit question. They were given a scale where 7 equaled a "superb" fit and one equaled a "terrible" fit. Their answers are summarized in exhibit 3.5.

The culture-environment fit in the case of the higher-performing firms was usually reported to be significantly better than in the cases of the other companies. On a seven-point scale, the higher-performing firms received scores averaging 6.1; the lower performers received a mean score of 3.7. Furthermore, not one of the ten lower performers received a score that was higher than the better performer(s) in its industry. Indeed, only one of them received a score that was both moderately high in an absolute sense and reasonably close to its higher-performing rivals. That firm was Archer Daniels Midland, the best per-

EXHIBIT 3.4

PERFORMANCE AND CULTURE/CONTEXT FIT

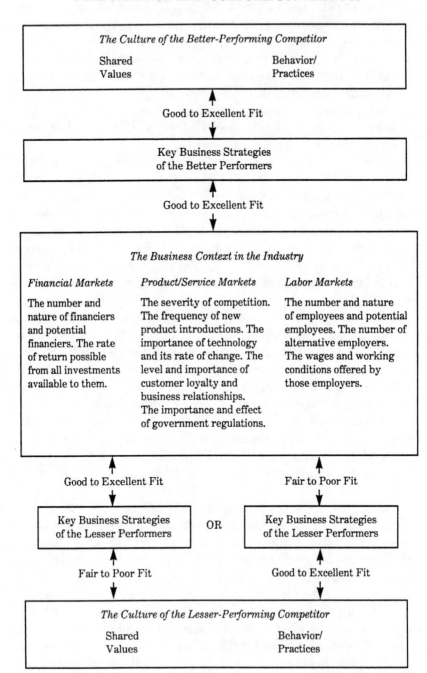

EXHIBIT 3.5

CULTURE/ENVIRONMENT FIT CIRCA 1977–1988*

Industry	The Twelve Higher Performers	Culture/ Environment Fit (7 = high, 1 = low)	The Ten Lower Performers	Culture/ Environment Fit (7 = high, 1 = low)
Airlines	American	6.2	Northwest	3.7
Banking	Bankers Trust	6.5	Citicorp	3.0
Beverages	Anheuser-Busch	6.4	Coors	2.2
	PepsiCo	5.5		
Office Equipment & Computers	Hewlett-Packard	5.7	Xerox	3.8
Food	ConAgra	6.4	Archer Daniels Midland	6.2
Oil	Shell	6.5	Texaco	2.6
Food & Drug Retailing	Albertsons	6.2	Winn-Dixie	3.0
Other Retailing	Dayton Hudson	4.4	J.C. Penney	4.1
	Wal-Mart	6.8		
Savings & Loan	Golden West	7.0	H.F. Ahmanson	5.0
Textiles	Springs Industries	5.3	Fieldcrest Cannon	3.6
	Mean	6.1	Mean	3.7

* Based on interviews with industry analysts described in exhibit A.9 in the Appendix.

former in the lower group. These results are clearly consistent with the strategically appropriate cultures perspective.

To test the validity of the results shown in exhibit 3.5 further, we took three actions. First, we personally visited thirteen of the twenty-two firms. Less formally, we interviewed current and former managers at four of the remaining nine companies (see exhibit A.12 for a list of the questions we asked).[9] We also showed the data in exhibit 3.5 to a few hundred senior managers who did not work for these firms but who were familiar with two or more of them. We uncovered little disagreement with the ratings made by our seventy-five financial analysts.

*   *   *

As we analyzed our interview data, we also looked for evidence that supported the major criticism of Theory II—that a good fit can be undermined by a changing environment and thus hurt long-term economic performance. That evidence was not difficult to find. Every one of the lower performers in our sample was reported to have had a significantly better culture/environment fit at an earlier time. Yet this fit had eroded, often as a result of changes to which these firms had not adapted.

Northwest Airlines is a dramatic example. Before deregulation in 1979, its cost-cutting, financially oriented strategy and culture were said to fit reasonably well in a highly regulated industry. After deregulation, its poor customer service, under increasingly competitive conditions, hurt its economic performance. Northwest's traditional labor-relations practices made it difficult to implement a new customer-service strategy. Ultimately, the only response that seemed viable to its financially oriented management was a major acquisition (Republic Airlines in 1986). But that action hurt performance even more for a few years because a huge effort had to be expended internally to merge the two organizations, especially union seniority lists. As a result, an airline that had earned nearly $430 million between 1973 and 1980 reported total profits of only slightly more than half that in the following seven-year period.

Changes in culture/environment fit usually evolved much more slowly in the other cases, but they clearly evolved. At Coors, when management decided to expand beyond their Rocky Mountain regional base, they encountered geographic areas with different subcultures, markets where they didn't have a strong reputation, and tougher competition. But their strong cowboy values were very slow to change, especially those associated with advertising ("a good product sells itself"), labor unions ("useless"), and debt ("borrow money and the banker will try to run your business"). As a result, the culture/environment misfits grew. Just as in the Donaldson/Lorsch research, those misfits were not quickly and easily brought back into alignment. The net result: performance suffered greatly; return on invested capital plunged from 12.9 percent in 1977 to 4.5 percent in 1988.

This theme of tougher competition helping to create culture/environment mismatches is pervasive in the cases of the lower performers. For Citicorp, that competition came from nonbank financial institutions, a less regulated banking industry, and the international expansion of foreign banks. For Xerox, the competitors came from Japan. In Winn-Dixie's case, other food retailers invaded their stronghold in the Southeast. For J.C. Penney, the increased competition came from both discounters and specialty stores. But whatever the source, in all these situations, the increased competition changed the business environment. Yet the cultures of these firms seemed to have had difficulty adapting to those changes. As a result, fit deteriorated and performance declined. See exhibit 3.6.

But why did the managers at these ten firms allow this to happen? No one can justly say they were stupid or uninformed. Xerox and Citicorp, for example, hired people from some of the nation's best schools and best companies. Managers at many of these companies were told by consultants that significant change was needed. Yet they still did not produce those needed changes. Although we will delay until Chapter 6 a complete exploration of this question, two points can be made here: (1) a culture can blind people to facts that don't match its assumptions, even very smart, experienced, and successful executives, and (2) an entrenched culture can make implementing new and different strategies very difficult.

From these cases, one might be tempted to believe that substantial cultural change is impossible—that perhaps there is a negative correlation between strength of culture and long-term economic performance. But the stories of the twelve better performers clearly do not support this interpretation.[10] All of the better performers had strong cultures; on a 1 (strong) to 5 (very weak) scale, their culture strength scores averaged 1.8.

EXHIBIT 3.6

THE CREATION AND IMPACT OF A STRATEGICALLY INAPPROPRIATE CULTURE

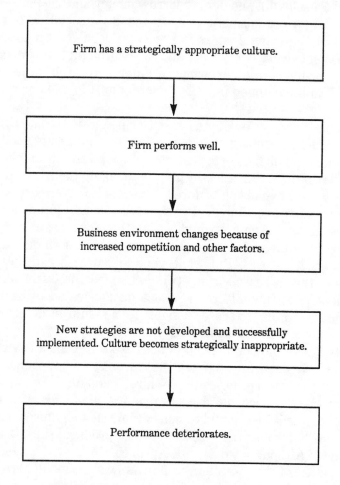

All were in situations that changed during the period under study. Albertson's, for example, grew dramatically, encountered new competition in its geographical expansion, and faced an array of new technological possibilities. Hewlett-Packard went through a major transformation from relying on an instrument-dominated product line to emphasizing a computer-dominated line. American Airlines faced the same deregulated environment that Northwest did. Dayton Hudson sold a significant number of its businesses. Golden West faced double-digit inflation and deregulation, both of which had a huge impact on the savings and loan industry. Anheuser-Busch had to deal with new strong competition from Miller. Yet each of these firms performed admirably. On average, the twelve better performers increased their net incomes over 18 percent per year during this eleven-year period. Their market values went up over 20 percent per year. All the evidence clearly suggests that, somehow, they successfully adapted to change, despite having reasonably strong cultures. Neither Theory II nor the strong-cultures-are-bad perspective can explain why these twelve adapted but their ten counterparts did not.

Nevertheless, Theory II also has some validity. Its primary concept, that of fit, appears to be useful—particularly in explaining differences in short- to medium-term performance. That concept also has important implications for firms in multiple businesses. It says that one uniform culture won't work; some variations are needed to fit the specific requirements of those different businesses.

But although this perspective can explain as much or more about culture and performance than Theory I can by itself, it still cannot account for all the cases in our research. In particular, it has no concept for explaining differential success at adapting to change, and hence, differences in long-term performance. For that, we must look again elsewhere.

4

ADAPTIVE CULTURES

There is a third perspective in the culture literature that speaks directly to the adaptation issue. The basic logic of Theory III is very straightforward: only cultures that can help organizations anticipate and adapt to environmental change will be associated with superior performance over long periods of time.

Proponents of this viewpoint often look at cultures that are not very adaptive for insight into what would constitute an adaptive culture. They note that nonadaptive cultures are usually very bureaucratic. People are reactive, risk averse, and not very creative. Information does not flow quickly and easily throughout the organization. A widespread emphasis on control dampens motivation and enthusiasm. Adaptive cultures, they conclude, must have very different characteristics.[1]

Ralph Kilmann describes such a culture in this way: "An adaptive culture entails a risk-taking, trusting, and proactive approach to organizational as well as individual life. Members actively support one another's efforts to identify all problems and implement workable solutions. There is a shared feeling of confidence: the members believe, without a doubt, that they can effectively manage whatever new problems and opportunities will come their way. There is widespread enthusiasm, a spirit of doing whatever it takes to achieve organizational success. The members are receptive to change and innovation."[2] Rosabeth Kanter argues that this kind of culture values and encourages entrepreneurship, which can help a firm adapt to a changing environment by allowing it to identify and exploit new opportunities.[3] Kotter's view is similar, only he stresses leadership rather than entrepreneurialism.[4] He argues that the primary function of leadership is to produce change, and if a culture encourages that activity throughout the hierarchy, it will produce a great deal of risk taking, initiative, communication, and motivation.

Most proponents of Theory III would point to Digital Equipment Corporation as an example of a firm with a culture that has promoted innovation, risk taking, candid discussions, entrepreneurship, and leadership at multiple levels in the hierarchy. They would argue that this culture has helped the firm adapt more successfully to the rapidly changing computer industry than companies, such as Burroughs or Honeywell, whose cultures have not encouraged risk taking and entrepreneurship. The superior adaptability, they believe, is a key reason why Digital has so thoroughly outperformed many other firms over the past two decades.

3M is also a favorite among Theory III advocates, perhaps because it more consciously than most companies tries to promote a culture that can deal with a changing world. Managers at 3M have tried, for some years now, to make a certain minimum percentage of sales come from relatively new products. The firm has a cultural norm of being willing to fund good development initiatives, even if they originate at the lower ranks in the organization. It prides itself on being willing to evaluate new ideas openly and then take prudent risks. In the process it creates important new businesses.

Firms like Digital and 3M do seem to confirm this perspective. But in its most popular versions, this viewpoint is also not without critics. They note that, unlike Theory II, Theory III cannot explain why a firm without a risk taking or entrepreneurial culture might do well over an extended period (because the culture fits the environment and the environment isn't changing). It is more troubling, they say, that this theory seems to overlook central questions: Risk taking for what? Adaptation to what? Innovation for what? The most common version of this perspective does not say, or answers these questions only in a very vague and abstract way (e.g., to solve problems). Many proponents of Theory III do not (apparently) consider these questions important. They seem to assume that as long as a corporate culture promotes change and is not overtly political, it will be adaptive and produce good long-term economic performance.

Critics of this perspective insist that this is not sensible, and for the same reason that Theory I fails: neither theory indicates that the specific *direction* in which a strong culture aligns people or a change-promoting culture points people should make a big difference. Their argument is that a culture that values change or flexibility, may, for example, be very unadaptive, because it could encourage people—even intelligent and nonpolitical people—to change everything, or the wrong things. Similarly, a culture that values leadership may generate leadership in the wrong direction.

Tom Peters is the most visible person who has offered a version of Theory III that deals with this problem. In what appears to be an explicit condemnation of traditional economic models and their exclusive focus on stockholders, Peters stresses "customers" and implies that if a culture values customers strongly, and creates change to serve customers' needs, it will help make an organization adaptive.[5] Kotter's latest book offers a variation on this theme.[6] He emphasizes the importance of all the constituencies that support a business, especially customers, stockholders, and employees. Kotter never states explicitly why a managerial culture needs to care about all of its key constituencies, but the implicit logic is this: only when managers care about the legitimate interests of stockholders do they strive to perform well economically over time, and in a competitive industry that is only possible when they take care of their customers, and in a competitive labor market, that is only possible when they take care of those who serve customers— employees. In other words, Kotter is saying that the relevant environment to which a management must adapt consists of its key constituencies. As a result, Kotter would argue that even a very entrepreneurial firm (like Digital) will not adapt successfully to change unless its managers strongly care about all key constituencies.

As was the case with Theories I and II, none of these versions of Theory III has been explicitly tested. Until now.

*   *   *

When interviewing industry analysts about our sample of twenty-two firms, we asked questions related to the core aspect of Theory III. Again, the results turned out to be very interesting.

When asked "How much does the culture (at some specific firm) value excellent leadership from its managers," interviewees replied as summarized in exhibit 4.1. On a scale of 1 (doesn't value leadership) to 7 (highly values leadership), the higher-performing firms received scores averaging 6.0. Not one was given a score lower than 4.8, and all but two scored higher than 5.5. The lower-performing firms did much worse. On average, they scored 3.9, with only two of these companies scoring higher than 4.8.

Furthermore, none of the lower performers scored higher than its matched rival(s) on this dimension. Only two even came close to equaling the better performer's score (Citicorp and H. F. Ahmanson), and both of these firms outperformed most of the others in their group. The majority of the lower performers scored significantly below their matched competitor(s)—6.0 for American versus 3.4 for Northwest, 6.6 for PepsiCo versus 2.5 for Coors, and so on.

Moreover, when describing how the cultures of the better performers had influenced their economic results, interviewees often referred to qualities such as leadership, entrepreneurship, prudent risk taking, candid discussions, innovation, and flexibility. Those were seen as cultural traits that helped the firms do well in a changing business environment. In other words, they saw a causal link going from cultures that value leadership and the other qualities mentioned above to superior performance—an assessment that is entirely consistent with the adaptive-cultures viewpoint.

When describing the lower performers, they used stodgier words such as "bureaucratic," or "emphasizes short-term results." These traits were seen as hurting performance in a changing business environment.

In terms of the purpose or direction of that leadership, the twelve better performing firms were reported to have had cultures that placed a high value on customers. On a 1 (low) to 7

EXHIBIT 4.1

CULTURAL VALUES RELATED TO LEADERSHIP*

The Higher-Performing Firms	Value Excellent Leadership (7 = absolutely yes, 1 = definitely not)	The Lower-Performing Firms	Value Excellent Leadership (7 = absolutely yes, 1 = definitely not)
American Airlines	6.0	Northwest Airlines	3.4
Bankers Trust	5.8	Citicorp	5.5
Anheuser-Busch	5.0	Coors	2.5
PepsiCo	6.6		
Hewlett-Packard	4.8	Xerox	3.8
ConAgra	6.8	Archer Daniels Midland	4.8
Shell	6.2	Texaco	3.0
Albertsons	6.6	Winn-Dixie	3.2
Dayton Hudson	6.0	J.C. Penney	4.2
Wal-Mart	6.8		
Golden West	5.6	H.F. Ahmanson	5.2
Springs Industries	5.7	Fieldcrest Cannon	3.1
Mean	6.0	Mean	3.9

* Based on interviews with industry analysts described in exhibit A.9 of Appendix.

(high) scale, the better performers received an average score of 6.0. The lowest score in this category was 4.8. The lower performing firms did much worse. Their average score was approximately 4.6. Only two of these ten firms scored higher than 5.0. Three received scores under 3.7. (See exhibit 4.2.)

The better performing firms were also said to value highly

EXHIBIT 4.2

CULTURAL VALUES RELATED TO SERVING CUSTOMERS, STOCKHOLDERS, AND EMPLOYEES*

(Scale: 7 = absolutely yes; 1 = definitely not)

THE HIGHER-PERFORMING FIRMS	Value Customers	Value Stockholders	Value Employees
American Airlines	6.4	4.6	5.8
Bankers Trust	4.8	6.2	5.0
Anheuser-Busch	6.4	5.0	5.0
PepsiCo	5.0	6.0	5.4
Hewlett-Packard	6.6	5.0	6.8
ConAgra	6.2	7.0	6.6
Shell	6.5	4.5	5.0
Albertsons	6.8	6.4	5.6
Dayton Hudson	5.5	5.0	4.8
Wal-Mart	7.0	6.8	7.0
Golden West	5.2	6.8	5.8
Springs Industries	6.0	5.0	6.7
Mean	6.0	5.7	5.8

THE LESSER-PERFORMING FIRMS	Value Customers	Value Stockholders	Value Employees
Northwest	3.6	4.9	2.8
Citicorp	5.0	3.3	3.0
Coors	3.6	1.5	4.2
Xerox	5.0	3.8	5.3
Archer Daniels Midland	5.6	6.0	5.2
Texaco	3.4	2.8	2.8
Winn-Dixie	4.0	4.0	4.0
J.C. Penney	4.0	5.0	4.8
H.F. Ahmanson	6.3	4.6	4.2
Fieldcrest Cannon	5.4	2.6	4.2
Mean	4.6	3.9	4.1

* Based on interviews with industry analysts described in exhibit A.9 of the Appendix.

their stockholder constituencies. On average, they scored 5.7. Only two were given scores lower than 5.0. The lower-performing firms did poorly here too—averaging 3.9, with only one company scoring higher than 5.0.

This pattern is maintained on the question of valuing employees. The higher-performers averaged 5.8. The very lowest score given here was 4.8. The lower performers averaged 4.1. Only two of these firms scored higher than 4.8.

In two cases (Citicorp and H.F. Ahmanson), lower-performing firms outscored their higher-performing counterparts on the "values customers" scale (in apparent contradiction to Peters's version of Theory III). In two cases (Northwest and J.C. Penney), lower-performing firms matched or surpassed their higher-performing counterparts on the "values stockholders" scale (in apparent contradiction to traditional economic models). In one case (J.C. Penney), the lower performer tied the score of its counterpart on the "values employees" scale. *But in no case did a lower performer receive a higher combined score.* In other words, valuing *all* key constituencies differentiates the better performers from the others.

This raises one more question. If the managers at the lower-performing firms do not value highly their customers, their stockholders, or their employees, what do they care about? When asked, our interviewees most often said: "Themselves."

Combining the scores on the "values leadership" scale (at exhibit 4.1) and the "values key constituencies" scale (at exhibit 4.2), again none of the lower performers outscored their rivals. In fact, in this case, no lower performer even came close to matching its counterpart. And those who trail their higher-performing counterparts by the smallest margins are consistently the best performers of the lower group.

Within the constraints of this methodology, the message from the data is clear. In the firms with more adaptive cultures, the cultural ideal is that managers throughout the hierarchy should provide leadership to initiate change in strategies and tactics whenever necessary to satisfy the legitimate interests of not just stockholders, or customers, or employees, but all three. In less adaptive cultures, the norm is that managers behave cautiously and politically to protect or advance themselves, their product, or their immediate work groups. (See exhibit 4.3.)

*   *   *

EXHIBIT 4.3

ADAPTIVE VS. UNADAPTIVE CORPORATE CULTURES

	Adaptive Corporate Cultures	Unadaptive Corporate Cultures
Core Values	Most managers care deeply about customers, stockholders, and employees. They also strongly value people and processes that can create useful change (e.g., leadership up and down the management hierarchy)	Most managers care mainly about themselves, their immediate work group, or some product (or technology) associated with that work group. They value the orderly and risk-reducing management process much more highly than leadership initiatives
Common Behavior	Managers pay close attention to all their constituencies, especially customers, and initiate change when needed to serve their legitimate interests, even if that entails taking some risks	Managers tend to behave somewhat insularly, politically, and bureaucratically. As a result, they do not change their strategies quickly to adjust to or take advantage of changes in their business environments

To explore these conclusions and to check the evaluations and opinions of our interviewees, we studied seventeen of the twenty-two firms in our sample in more depth. To do so, we formally visited thirteen of these firms and interviewed employees and executives (our interview guide is in exhibit A.10). Less formally, we interviewed managers employed at four of the other companies as opportunity permitted.[7]

As a general rule, we found much more evidence of cultures that have supported change at the higher-performing firms than at the lower. Precisely what engine of change was emphasized varied. In most cases it was leadership throughout the management hierarchy. But sometimes it was strong leadership at the top, sometimes it was risk taking, sometimes it was entrepreneurship, occasionally it was innovation or flexibility. Whatever the case, one thing was very clear; the higher performers simply looked, felt, and sounded more active than the lower performers. Occasionally, this was striking, as when a divisional personnel manager at ConAgra described, with pride, an entrepreneurial scheme he was devising to offer relocation services to his managers for the move of the division's headquarters to a new city. His idea called for the creation of a temporary group inside Con-Agra to provide these services and for exploiting certain advantages that an inside group would have so as to offer high quality services at a considerably lower cost than if he hired an outside firm specializing in relocation.

We also found considerably more evidence at the higher performers of a value system that really cared about all key constituencies. Which constituencies were stressed the most varied: stockholders at ConAgra and Golden West, customers at Albertson's and Anheuser-Busch, employees at Hewlett-Packard and Springs Industries. But no group was ignored, and fairness to everyone was a standard feature—a commitment often described as an emphasis on "integrity" or "doing the right thing."

Again, this was sometimes striking. At Albertson's, there was a "Corporate Creed" stating the firm's responsibility to customers, employees, community, shareholders, and society. At ConAgra, something similar was written in four-inch-high letters on a wall near the executive offices. At Dayton Hudson, we found the same proclamation in its "statement of philosophy." At Anheuser-Busch, the commitment to constituencies was in its "mission statement." At Springs Industries, the very first line of its 1989 annual report is "Springs enters the 1990s well prepared to serve our customers, our people, and our shareholders." PepsiCo's 1988 annual report opens with a similar statement. At American Airlines, a strong commitment to all their constituencies was written in its statement of "Corporate Vision."

Although a few of the lower performers had somewhat similar statements, these tended to be more recent and to list fewer key constituencies. Often they seemed artificial, as though they were the product of a single individual or a single meeting, and not the real priorities of most managers. At the lower-performing firms, managers seemed to care more about either their own careers or perks or specific products and technologies.

Evidence of adaptability—of useful change—was again much easier to find at the better performers, especially in areas in which the business environment has been most turbulent. Albertson's, for example, was not founded by technologists, had few engineers in senior management, yet had done an excellent job of adapting to changing computer technology—a conclusion that was substantiated not only by the machines we found at its check-out stands, but by the weekly computer printout we saw almost all their executives *using*. The situation looked different at Winn-Dixie. At ConAgra, not only were PC's in executive offices but executives actually made use of this equipment on a regular basis (more so than at Archer Daniels Midland). Effective adaptation to changing computer technology was but one aspect of the story at American Airlines. Faced with a drastic change in its industry, American literally made hundreds of changes in the early 1980s; the firm cut costs, created hubs, altered routes, rewrote labor contracts, grounded a whole fleet of 707s, invented frequent flyer programs, automated processes, and consolidated functions and facilities (much more useful change than one finds during the same period at Northwest). To win against competition that began offering products aimed at segmented customer groups, Anheuser-Busch managers more than tripled the number of different beers they sold in the 1980s (usually changing faster and more successfully than Coors).

It was more difficult to find hard evidence of causality: *from* a culture that supports leadership and values all constituencies *to* adaptability. But that evidence certainly exists; it simply is not as visible. Hewlett-Packard is perhaps the clearest single example, and one we will describe at some length in the next chapter. In general, though, the pattern seems to be this. When managers care deeply about their main constituencies, they pay close attention to those constituencies. When something in the firm's context changes—such as the level of competition— managers are quick to spot this trend. If they also believe strongly in the importance of leadership at multiple levels in the hierarchy, they then provide that leadership to reduce their costs, to improve their products, or to do whatever else might be appropriate in the given situation. If changes in the firm's strategies and practices are needed in order to respond to new contextual conditions, even practices rooted in the culture, those initiatives continue until the cultural changes are made. In this way, managers help maintain a fit between the culture and its context (see exhibit 4.4).

EXHIBIT 4.4

HOW ADAPTIVE CULTURES WORK

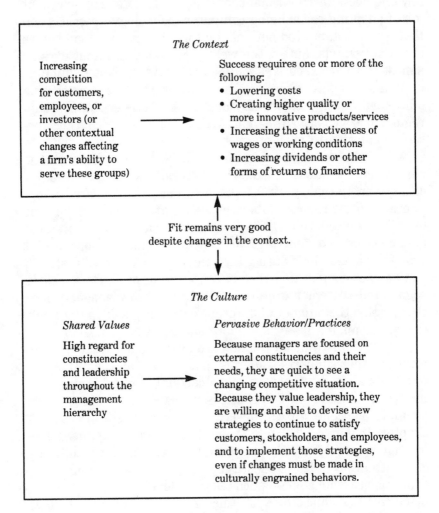

The Context

Increasing competition for customers, employees, or investors (or other contextual changes affecting a firm's ability to serve these groups)

Success requires one or more of the following:
- Lowering costs
- Creating higher quality or more innovative products/services
- Increasing the attractiveness of wages or working conditions
- Increasing dividends or other forms of returns to financiers

Fit remains very good despite changes in the context.

The Culture

Shared Values

High regard for constituencies and leadership throughout the management hierarchy

Pervasive Behavior/Practices

Because managers are focused on external constituencies and their needs, they are quick to see a changing competitive situation. Because they value leadership, they are willing and able to devise new strategies to continue to satisfy customers, stockholders, and employees, and to implement those strategies, even if changes must be made in culturally engrained behaviors.

When managers do not care about all three key constituencies and about leadership initiatives throughout the management hierarchy, the net result always seems to be less effective adaptation. This is perhaps most obvious when a high concern for customers and/or leadership is lacking. But this is also true in a firm with a strong customer orientation but without much concern for employees or stockholders. In such cases, managers try hard to meet customers' changing needs, even if that means significantly reducing margins and working employees very long hours. That strategy sometimes works well for a while, but eventually capital becomes too scarce to invest much in needed new products or services. Furthermore, employees start to feel exploited and stop working hard for the customer. As a result, such firms find it harder and harder to meet changing customer requirements.

*   *   *

An important question that arises from this study is: how did our twelve higher-performing firms develop and maintain their relatively adaptive cultures? Answering that question in detail goes beyond the scope of our research, but during our visits to the higher-performing firms we noticed certain shared characteristics that provide some insight into this issue.

The adaptive cultures at these companies all seem to have originated around a small number of people, often just one person: Adolphus Busch at Anheuser-Busch, C. R. Smith at American Airlines, Sam Walton at Wal-Mart, Marion and Herb Sandler at Golden West, Charlie Sanford at Bankers Trust, Don Kendall (and possibly Andy Pearson) at PepsiCo, Bill Hewlett and Dave Packard at Hewlett-Packard, Mike Harper at ConAgra, Joe Albertson at Albertson's, the Daytons at Dayton Hudson, and Elliot Springs at Springs Industries. These individuals and their management teams developed strategies that fit the business environments in which they operated, that worked well and, as a result, became embedded in the cultures of their firms. But the same can be said for most, if not all, of the lower performers. What seems to differentiate the two groups is this: in the cases of the better performers, the leaders got their managers to buy into a timeless philosophy or set of values that stressed both meeting constituency needs and leadership or some other engine for change—values that cynics would liken to motherhood, but that when followed can be very powerful. Those people and their successors then perpetuated the adaptive part of their cultures—the values/philosophy part relating to constituencies and leadership—because they worked at it.

In most cases this cultural preservation was conscious and deliberate. Warren McCann, the CEO at Albertson's, calls himself "the custodian of the corporate culture." John Young, the CEO at Hewlett-Packard, told us that he has an important role to play in "preserving the firm's core values." Ken Macke, CEO at Dayton Hudson, said he spends 40 percent of his time teaching others, and a key part of the curriculum is cultural.

Executives at the higher-performing firms helped perpetuate adaptive values by talking about them and writing about them. August Busch, the current CEO at Anheuser-Busch, has found time to address groups that include every single employee, all 32,000 of them, at least once a year, and to answer their questions. Many former or current CEOs of the twelve higher-performing firms have worked with their managers to publish and circulate statements about their core values. Most also have used symbolic communication: CEO Walter Elisha has commissioned a set of large sculptures to represent the core values at Springs Industries. Bob Crandall and his people at American Airlines have done something similar with the design of the lobby at their new headquarters in Dallas, an architecture that virtually screams "we care about customer service" (there is a ticket office in the lobby), "we keep our costs down" (there is a telephone instead of a receptionist), "and we are striving to be more global" (on the wall there is a huge map of the world showing the cities American currently serves).

These people also have successfully perpetuated the adaptive part of their cultures by behaving in ways consistent with those values. Most, like CEOs Mike Harper at ConAgra or Marion Sandler at Golden West, are living and breathing role models of what their companies stand for. Even in crisis they have rarely been caught in the culture-destroying trap of saying one thing and then doing another.

These executives have hired and promoted people who have values consistent with those that are core in their cultures. They have not demanded blind conformity to their own personal philosophies; on the contrary, many seem to have valued diversity in their management ranks. But if a subordinate clearly violated a core cultural value (such as failing to encourage leadership), even if he or she performed well by certain quantifiable measures, these executives were often willing to sanction that person severely.[8]

As their firms grew and added formal systems, these executives ensured that those systems reinforced adaptive values. They were usually quick to spot a proposed compensation system or performance appraisal process that would not reflect the core philosophy of the firm. They seem to have been especially

EXHIBIT 4.5

HOW ADAPTIVE CULTURES ARE DEVELOPED AND PRESERVED

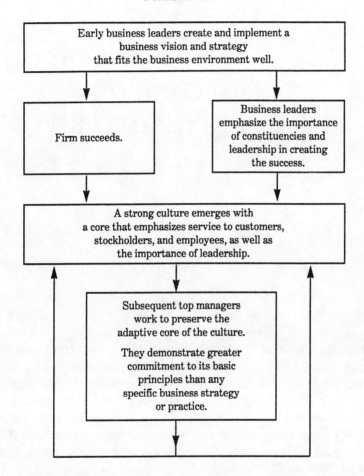

alert to the danger of unwanted changes to the heart of the culture, no matter what the source. In this way they stopped or reversed trends toward creeping arrogance or insularity that easily can be the product of great success.

As a result of all these efforts, even though their organizations were always changing—with new (potentially cynical) people being hired and promoted—the adaptive core of their cultures lived on. And in this way, their leadership on the issue of culture helped promote excellent long-term economic performance (see exhibit 4.5).

5

THE CASE OF
HEWLETT-PACKARD

Although none of the three theoretical perspectives on corporate culture and performance is entirely satisfying, all provide important insights into why some firms are doing better than others today. The strong-cultures model (Theory I) shows the role that norms and values can play in aligning, motivating, and controlling a group of people, tasks that can be enormously difficult in complex organizations. The strategically appropriate cultures model (Theory II) demonstrates the importance of having practices that fit the specific conditions in which a culture operates. The adaptation model (Theory III) highlights specific values and behaviors that can help a firm and its culture adapt to change.

Although each of these perspectives is usually discussed as an alternative to the others, there is nothing inherently conflicting in them. Indeed, our research suggests that a model combining all three perspectives is more powerful than any of them separately.

This new perspective is summarized visually in exhibit 5.1. It says that a corporate culture will enhance a firm's long-term

EXHIBIT 5.1

A PERFORMANCE-ENHANCING CORPORATE CULTURE

Shared Managerial Values

Almost all managers care strongly about people who have a stake in the
business—customers, employees, stockholders, suppliers, etc. They also
value leadership or other processes that can produce change.

Managerial Behavior Norms

Managers engage in practices that fit a sensible strategy for the business
context (i.e., the needs and expectations of key constituencies). When
necessary, they provide leadership to create and implement new
strategies and practices to maintain a good fit. They also seek, train, and
promote individuals who behave in a similar way and (perhaps more
important) share their core values.

economic performance if the managers care deeply about their
customers, their stockholders, and their employees, as well as
leadership and other processes that can produce change. With
this value system, managers will pay close attention to their
constituencies and then create and implement strategies that
are sensible in light of constituency needs. Satisfied employees
will be directed and encouraged to produce products (and services) that customers really want, and to do so using financial
assets wisely. These actions will help the organization grow,
while allowing margins to grow or remain high, which, in turn,
will increase net income and market value, while increasing net
income as a percent of invested capital.

The values of a culture of this kind may sound commonplace
to some, but they are far from the norm today. In most firms,
managers do not care deeply about customers *and* stockholders
and employees.[1] They may value strongly one of their constituency groups, or perhaps even two, but not all three. More
likely, they have been taught to care more about their kind of
work (accounting, engineering, etc.), their department, specific
products, or only themselves. Nor do most managers today believe in the importance of leadership at multiple levels in the
firm. Many have even been taught that multiple leadership initiatives inevitably create chaos.

Hewlett-Packard is a good example of a firm that embodies

this new perspective. According to the analysts we interviewed, the adaptive capacity of HP's culture has been typical of our twelve better performers; its combined constituency and leadership score ranked it sixth in the group of twelve. That capacity was tested severely in the 1970s and 1980s. During that period, HP's situation changed considerably, creating a stream of performance-degrading misfits (or potential misfits) between the corporate culture and the firm's context. But despite the strength of HP's culture (rated at 1.9 on a 1 = high to 5 = low scale), it managed to adapt sufficiently well to keep the firm's performance in the very good to excellent range. The key to that successful adaptation can be found in HP's core philosophy and values.

*   *   *

Hewlett-Packard was founded in 1939 as a partnership of two Stanford University electrical engineers—Bill Hewlett and Dave Packard—who worked out of a rented garage in Palo Alto, California.[2] Their first product was an audio oscillator that provided higher performance at a lower price than competing instruments. Subsequent products followed this same strategy: high quality, innovative electronic instruments aimed at scientific and engineering markets. In 1942, with sixty employees, HP built a 10,000 square foot office. In 1943, sales nearly passed the $1 million mark. In 1947, growth required a second new building, and by the end of that decade, the firm was introducing twenty new products each year. Sales topped $15 million in 1955 and $60 million in 1960.

During these early years, Hewlett, Packard, and their associates developed a philosophy about how to run a business and a style of operations that subsequently became known as "the HP way." For a variety of reasons, this philosophy became embedded in a very strong and powerful culture: in part because Hewlett and Packard shared some basic values from the beginning, but also because they hired and promoted like-minded people, because their business success reinforced their business strategies and style of operations, and because they explicitly communicated key aspects of the HP way to their employees, an example being their 1957 statement of "Corporate Objectives."

Like most strong cultures, this "HP way" was complex and not easy to describe. In terms of basic values, it stressed serving everyone who had a stake in the business with integrity and fairness. The HP way meant that the firm shared its success with its employees, recognizing their individual achievements, offering them opportunities to upgrade their skills and abilities, and always showing them trust and respect. The HP way meant providing the firm's customers products and services of the greatest value, usually unique or technically superior products, and being genuinely interested in arriving at effective solutions to their problems. The HP way also meant serving the firm's stockholders by making profit a high priority and not getting into businesses where HP could not make a profitable contribution. For society in general, it meant being a very good corporate citizen.

The core values at HP also gave a priority to self-financing growth (i.e., no long-term debt), initiative, creativity, and managers who engender enthusiasm and teamwork throughout the organization.

In terms of more specific practices, the HP way included management-by-wandering-around, informal collegial behavior, some form of management-by-objectives, an avoidance of layoffs, innovating in "bite sizes," minimizing acquisitions, and not buying market share. It also stressed that managers should create an open-architecture office structure, fully integrated and autonomous operating units, a minimum of bureaucracy, and comfortable work environments.

These values and methods of operating directed employees in ways that fit HP's business environment and thus motivated great achievements. They helped the firm to attract still more employees, to satisfy an increasing number of customers, to make money, and to grow.

By any reasonable measure, HP's performance in the 1950s and 1960s was excellent: net income increased 107 times during that period. The market value of the firm increased 5.6 times between 1957 and 1967. Return on invested capital averaged over 15 percent. Although many factors contributed to these results, Bill Hewlett and Dave Packard were convinced that the HP culture was one of the most important of all. The senior employees agreed; many loved the culture and believed it should be preserved at all costs. And never change.

*   *   *

The business environment in which Hewlett-Packard operated was never static. But the 1970s and 1980s saw the advent of changes more fundamental in nature than ever before in the company's history. The firm shifted its strategic focus from instruments to computers, with the latter accounting for two-thirds of sales in 1990. Stand-alone products gave way to modular systems of interconnected components. The firm moved into a much more competitive market environment. It grew from a medium-sized company to a very large corporation, with 1989 revenues of nearly $12 billion. And on top of all this, the very visible founders retired to the Board of Directors and turned the reins over to a new management team.

Each change was accompanied or followed by a few cultural changes. Viewed in isolation, most of these changes do not seem significant. But taken together, they represent substantial alterations, especially given the general tendency for a strong culture to resist change.

The computer business gave rise to a new subculture that did not stress small, self-contained subunits. In that subculture, strategy was set at higher levels. Some business functions were not put in the divisions. Cowboy entrepreneurs were somewhat less valued. Administrative functions were sometimes much more consolidated. Marketing gained power, especially relative to Research and Development. Distribution channels were used other than the traditional HP sales force. In the eyes of some observers, these changes alone made HP a very different company in 1990 than it was in 1975. But these computer-related shifts represented only one part of the total picture.

In the increasingly competitive business environment, an even higher standard of quality became the norm in most parts of the firm. A variety of less paternalistic (cradle to grave) employment practices came into being; in 1986, HP offered early retirement for the first time ever, and in 1989, after acquiring Apollo Computer, it laid off employees there on three different occasions.

As the company grew, the culture at HP tolerated more specialization. Seat-of-the-pants approaches to business became rare. For a while, the company became bureaucratic, with much less management-by-walking-around and the extreme use of committees; this trend was reversed in 1990. When the founders retired, the leadership of the organization began to take on the look of "professional management"—somewhat less visible and powerful, more consensual in decision making.

Few of these changes came easily. Typically, the prospect of some alternative practice was greeted by cries of "No, that's not the HP way." In some cases, the arguments were loud and long. Even today, many senior employees are still not happy with what has happened.

It is possible to argue, as do long-term service employees, that these changes are not all for the good. But the new culture is, for the most part, a logical response to a new set of conditions (see exhibit 5.2). It may not represent a perfect fit with HP's current business environment; the analysts we interviewed didn't think it was. But it is clearly a reasonable fit with the new circumstances, and one that is superior, in this regard, to the old culture.

But why wasn't the old culture more resistant to change? Why didn't those arguing against abolishing old HP practices win the day? When we asked HP treasurer George Newman these questions, he said:

EXHIBIT 5.2

CHANGE AT HEWLETT-PACKARD

HP's Business Context	*HP's Culture*
A change from mostly instrument products to mostly computer products (with accompanying changes in size and integration of products, in the amount of competition, nature of customers, etc.). A change from a medium to a large firm. A shift from entrepreneurial top managers to more "professional" management. A general change to a tougher and more competitive business enviroment.	*Common Behavior* • Fewer small and self-contained subunits created. • Strategy set at higher levels. • Distribution channels used other than HP sales force. • More effort at creating quality (to satisfying customer needs). • Less paternalistic personnel practices. • More consensual decision making at the top. • The use of somewhat more specialized and bureaucratic structures. *Shared Values* • Cowboy entrepreneurs less valued. • In general, fewer changes here than in the behaviorial aspects of culture.

I think a lot of it had to do with the kinds of objectives that Hewlett and Packard made central to the culture many years ago. They weren't very specific. Instead they represented more of a general philosophy of how to be successful—a timeless philosophy that talks about the value of profit, satisfied customers, a good environment for employees, and the like. I think our collective commitment to those principles has helped us adapt to a changing world much more successfully than firms that have, as core values, such things as "maintain an AA bond rating."

I think it also helps that our culture encourages people to step up to the plate. It encourages us to have a radical idea every once in a while. That helps to keep us from getting too set in our ways.[3]

Ned Barnholt, general manager of the Electronic Instruments Group, answers the same questions this way:

A part of our culture has stressed innovation and entrepreneurship, and that has surely helped us to be adaptive over the years. That culture has also said we must be close to our customers in order to serve them well, and that has helped with adaptation too.

Let me give you an example. The original HP culture was a promote-from-within culture. We altered this practice somewhat when we went into computers. Why? To do well in computers (and our principles say we are not to enter businesses in which we can't do well and make money) and to serve the customers well, you have to have people who know that business and the customers of that business. We didn't have enough HP managers who did. So we had to go outside and bring in quite a few people. Although not everybody was happy with that decision, most of us recognized it was the right thing to do.[4]

In 1987, in response to some of the battles at HP over cultural change, CEO John Young requested that a project be established to examine the HP way. The project team interviewed managers and employees. It eventually created materials to help managers talk about the HP way with employees, especially new recruits. These materials differentiate three aspects of the culture: organizational values, corporate objectives, and strategies and policies. Project leader Lisa Shupp explains:

> We found it was useful to distinguish those aspects of the culture that were more central and less subject to change from those that were less central and more subject to change. If you look at our history, our basic values seem to change very little over the years. What we call our corporate objectives change in small ways every decade, but not a lot. But when you get to the level of specific strategies and practices, you find a considerable amount of change. That does not necessarily happen easily, but it does happen when circumstances make it necessary.[5]

CEO John Young speaks even more graphically about the importance of the 1987 project:

> Increasingly, we found ourselves in prolonged discussions about things that were thought by some to be important to our culture, the HP way. It wasn't until we sat down to sort out our core values that it became clear that the company picnic, for example, was only a means of serving core values that could be served just as well or better by other means. That project helped clear the air so we could proceed with necessary changes in strategies and practices so long as they reflected the basic values of the company.[6]

What these executives are saying is this: As relevant aspects of HP's business environments have changed, parts of HP's culture have also changed to maintain some minimum logical fit. That change has occurred because of more central (and less changing and less specific) aspects of the culture. That core set of values and behaviors keeps people focused on the firm's key constituencies and supports the kind of initiative and leadership that can create change. As a result, when the needs of constituencies (customers, employees, owners, and others) change, or when something happens that affects the firm's capacity to continue to meet those needs, leadership initiatives emerge to change the strategies and practices to fit environmental realities. When these initiatives come from middle or lower levels in the firm, they are usually supported by more senior managers because they share the values that motivated the initiatives in the first place. Because culture does not change easily, and because HP managers don't all care as deeply about stockholders and leadership as they do about customers and employees, adjustment occasions some anguish. But it usually occurs nevertheless.

The net result is that Hewlett-Packard has performed well over the long term. It has usually performed well in the short term as well, although not always. Cultural change always requires some time. During those periods of adjustment, some degree of poor cultural fit has reduced the firm's performance. If the new theory summarized in this chapter is correct, HP will continue to do well in the future unless something weakens its core adaptive values and behaviors or unless its business environment begins to change even faster without a corresponding increase in the strength of that adaptive core.

*   *   *

The general pattern found in the Hewlett-Packard case can also be seen in all the other better-performing firms in our study. Ask executives at Dayton Hudson if their corporate culture has changed in the last decade and most say that it has, but not much. Ask what aspects of the culture have not changed, and they talk mostly about very basic values, many of which they trace back to the Dayton family: such as commitment to the community, to customers, to consistent financial performance, to employees, and to innovation guided by "trend management." Ask them what has changed in the last ten years, and they speak of more specific practices: how the firm has become less formal and more candid, how the corporate focus has shifted to substantive business issues and away from the management process. Ask them if these changes are appropriate, and they describe other changes in the business environment. Ask them how these changes came about, and they talk about the leadership of CEO Ken Macke, a thirty-year veteran of Dayton Hudson. Macke himself admits that these and other changes did not occur easily, particularly those involving new businesses and divestitures. To bring about these changes, he says he had to talk "a lot about values, values that people around here care about," values that helped justify that the changes were needed.[7]

For the most part, the cultural dynamics at all twelve of the better performers were similar to those at Dayton Hudson and Hewlett-Packard. These cultures contributed to performance because they helped energize and align employees to a set of strategies and practices that fit the objective conditions of their situations, and because they had some built-in capacity to alter those strategies and practices when relevant conditions changed. As a result, the twelve firms significantly outperformed other competitors with equally strong but less adaptive cultures. They also outperformed rivals with weak cultures, for reasons inherent in the logic of Theory I; that is, they were much more able to energize employees and align their actions in reasonable directions. Not all twelve firms fit this generalization perfectly. But all appear closer to this pattern than any of the ten "lower performers."

We don't have the breadth of information needed to begin to test whether these performance-enhancing cultures are the single most important factor in the success of those firms—more important, for example, than the structure of an industry or the quality of top management. But the importance of culture to performance seems very clear from the data we do have.

This conclusion raises a number of issues. We address these next.

6

THE NATURE OF
LOW-PERFORMANCE
CULTURES

Our research on the relationship between corporate culture and long-term economic performance raises a number of interesting questions. What circumstances lead to the development of cultures that undermine economic performance? How frequently does this happen, and thus, how serious are the collective consequences of these cultures? How difficult is it to transform those cultures into ones that enhance performance, and why is this so?

To answer the first question, we studied the histories of twenty firms, none of which appear to have had cultures during the late 1970s and early 1980s resembling those we found to enhance economic performance:[1] H.F. Ahmanson, Avon, BankAmerica, Citicorp, Coors, Eastern Airlines, Fieldcrest Cannon, First Chicago, Ford, General Motors, Goodyear, K Mart, Kroger, Navistar, Northwest Airlines, PanAm, J.C. Penney, Sears, Texaco, and Xerox. For some economic performance data on these firms, see exhibit 6.1. Additional information can be found in exhibit A.11.

EXHIBIT 6.1

THE SAMPLE OF FIRMS USED FOR THE THIRD STUDY
(1977–1988)

COMPANY	Performance Index* Based on Net Income Growth STRONG** PERFORMANCE = 27–170	Average Yearly Return (%) on Invested Capital STRONG** PERFORMANCE = 13–40	Average Yearly Increase (%) in Stock Price STRONG** PERFORMANCE = 17–47
H.F. Ahmanson	12.4	4.49	12.80
Avon	7.0	18.94	−8.51
BankAmerica	5.8	4.97	−0.18
Citicorp	18.2	4.98	10.30
Coors	9.2	7.69	4.20
Eastern Airlines	−86.1	−0.44	14.69
Fieldcrest Cannon	8.3	5.64	6.40
First Chicago	10.7	5.55	8.76
Ford	12.0	11.40	14.82
General Motors	9.2	10.59	3.27
Goodyear	17.0	6.72	8.21
K Mart	15.6	9.19	8.72
Kroger	22.0	8.10	6.09
Navistar	−13.4	−2.36	4.94
Northwest Airlines	10.3	5.24	10.65
PanAm	−420.8	−10.90	3.96
J.C. Penney	16.0	8.90	10.65
Sears	14.8	7.19	5.87
Texaco	9.9	5.36	4.70
Xerox	13.1	8.86	4.30

* See exhibit A.4 for an explanation of the measure.
** Strong Performance = top quartile of all scores

These organizations represent a diverse cross section of industries and geographical locations within the United States; yet there seems to be an amazingly consistent pattern in the sequence of events that helped shape an important part of all their cultures. This pattern is different in at least one or two crucial respects from that found in the histories of the twelve higher performing firms discussed earlier.

The histories of these firms usually begin with some combination of visionary leadership and/or luck in which a good business strategy was implemented by a committed group of people. Because the strategy worked exceptionally well, it propelled these firms into strong positions in some market or markets and provided them with the means of sustaining that position. Some firms controlled important patents (Xerox); some enjoyed unique economies of scale (GM and Sears); some were protected by regulations limiting competition (Northwest on its Pacific routes); some had customers with strong brand loyalty (Coors). It seems that the positions the twenty firms in exhibit 6.1 achieved were, on average, stronger than the positions achieved by the twelve better-performing companies. This dominance, or the lack of competition associated with it, brought these firms great success in terms of both growth and profitability over a period of years during which they experienced little real adversity. But sustained growth created huge internal challenges: more and more employees were hired; the organizations grew larger and larger; day to day operations became more and more complex. To cope with the internal organizational challenges, executives sought, hired, developed, and promoted skilled managers who were not necessarily leaders—that is, people who understood structures and systems and budgets and controls much better than they did vision and strategies and culture and inspiration.[2] In time these individuals became top executives (see exhibit 6.2). With the changes in personnel, the relative ease with which these people were able to create revenue and profit growth given the strong market position, and the behavior of top management, any collective sense of why the firm was successful in the first place was lost along the way.

The unhealthy cultures that emerged from this scenario appear to have three general components. First, managers tended to be arrogant. At Texaco, for example, no one was ever encouraged to look outside the firm for superior business ideas;

EXHIBIT 6.2

COMMON CHANGES IN EXECUTIVE RANKS THAT BOTH
ACCOMPANY AND HELP CREATE THE EMERGENCE OF
UNADAPTIVE CORPORATE CULTURES

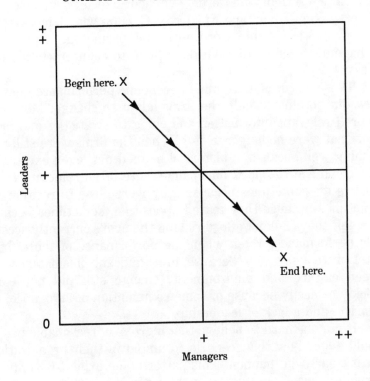

managers acted as if they already had all the answers.[3] This behavior appears to be the product of sustained success over a number of years with few if any clear failures and with little effort from top management to keep people realistically humble. Second, often in spite of public protestations to the contrary, managers in these cultures tended not to value highly customers *and* stockholders *and* employees. The response at Coors to customer complaints about a newly designed can top is typical: "We have heard that some customers have had problems opening the cans," the firm told its distributors. "But since we produce the best beer available, we are confident that our customers will find a way to get to it."[4] This extraordinary statement shows the arrogance that can grow where external pressures are low and top management is indifferent to the company's constituencies.

Third, these cultures became hostile to values such as leadership or other engines of change—in part because not much leadership was needed under the circumstances and partly because these firms had very strong managerial orientations, a perspective that values stability and order. Indeed, executives at General Motors, Winn-Dixie, and Fieldcrest Cannon who demonstrated "too much" leadership were often not promoted.[5] Again, top management seems to have done little to counteract this tendency.

These cultures undermined economic performance because they did nothing to help the firms adapt to change. Managers ignored relevant information and clung to strategies and practices that were no longer useful. When the firms were still performing well because of historical momentum, even executives who could see the need for change were often reluctant to introduce it—sometimes because they were close to retirement, sometimes because they feared opposition, sometimes because they felt they couldn't afford risking the firm's currently acceptable performance. Even when the performance of these firms deteriorated severely because of significant mismatches between culture and environment, change still did not come quickly or easily because of some combination of arrogance, insularity, and a lack of leadership.

It may be hard to believe that a group of reasonable people would ever allow this scenario to unfold in their organization, but it clearly did happen. This pattern (see exhibit 6.3) fits, in varying degrees, all twenty of the firms in our third study.

*   *   *

In many ways, the Xerox case is an extreme example of this phenomenon. It is also one of the most extraordinary stories in American business.[6]

Xerox was founded in 1906 by four Rochester, New York, businessmen as the Haloid Corporation. The firm manufactured photographic paper in a city dominated by Kodak. After a financial crisis in 1912, Haloid grew slowly but profitably for the next twenty years and then survived the Depression by introducing in 1933 the best photocopying paper then on the market. In 1935, the firm went public and used its new financing to buy a company that manufactured a camera designed specifically to photograph documents. During World War II, the firm worked at capacity to supply the Signal Corps, the Air Corps, and other

EXHIBIT 6.3

THE ORIGINS OF UNHEALTHY CORPORATE CULTURES

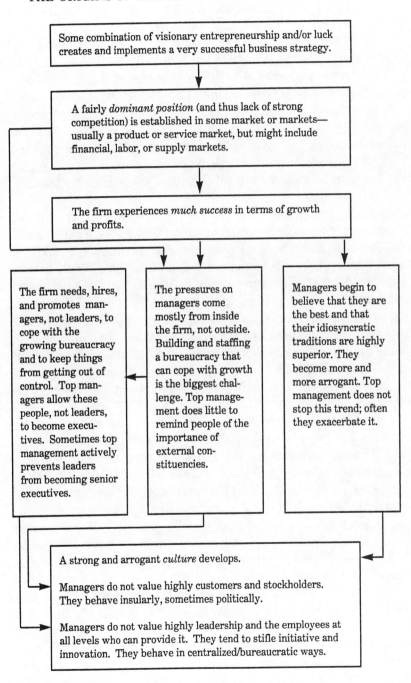

Some combination of visionary entrepreneurship and/or luck creates and implements a very successful business strategy.

A fairly *dominant position* (and thus lack of strong competition) is established in some market or markets— usually a product or service market, but might include financial, labor, or supply markets.

The firm experiences *much success* in terms of growth and profits.

The firm needs, hires, and promotes managers, not leaders, to cope with the growing bureaucracy and to keep things from getting out of control. Top managers allow these people, not leaders, to become executives. Sometimes top management actively prevents leaders from becoming senior executives.

The pressures on managers come mostly from inside the firm, not outside. Building and staffing a bureaucracy that can cope with growth is the biggest challenge. Top management does little to remind people of the importance of external constituencies.

Managers begin to believe that they are the best and that their idiosyncratic traditions are highly superior. They become more and more arrogant. Top management does not stop this trend; often they exacerbate it.

A strong and arrogant *culture* develops.

Managers do not value highly customers and stockholders. They behave insularly, sometimes politically.

Managers do not value highly leadership and the employees at all levels who can provide it. They tend to stifle initiative and innovation. They behave in centralized/bureaucratic ways.

branches of the military interested in surveillance. When the grandson of one of the four founders of the business was elected president in 1945, Haloid was nearly forty years old but had yearly revenues of less than $7 million.

That young man was Joe Wilson. His efforts to find fields of potential growth for Haloid led him in 1946 to Chet Carlson and electrophotography. Carlson had been developing this new technology for nearly a decade, but had failed totally in his attempts to obtain the interest and financial backing of corporations such as IBM, RCA, and A.B. Dick. Wilson was impressed enough by what he saw and heard that he negotiated limited rights to the inventor's work and patents and committed his firm to a path that led fourteen years later to the first "Xerox machine."

It was not an easy journey. Funding was often very tight; a government research grant of $120,000 was a lifesaver early on. The company's first xerographic office product, the Model A copier, failed because customers found it far too difficult to use. This could have killed xerography at Haloid had they not found a different but very profitable application for the Model A: making paper masters for offset duplicating. Many people questioned the firm's commitment to an undeveloped technology and its belief about the size of the potential office market for good copiers, but Joe Wilson's vision, tenacity, and capacity for shrewd decisions kept the company from dropping out or changing its course.

In 1947, Haloid took steps to increase its control of the xerographic patents held by others; by 1956, it successfully obtained ownership of all the key Carlson inventions. The firm also began to spend more and more on research and development to create its own patents. To help fund all this, the company aggressively added to its traditional product line a number of non-xerographic products. The Photographic Foto-Flo Recorder and the Foto-Flo Model C Photo-Copying Machine were two of the first. More of these non-xerographic products followed in the late 1940s and early 1950s.

In 1955, Haloid used a $3 million loan to build its first factory devoted to xerographic products. In that year the firm also expanded its R&D staff to 120 and introduced three new and improved types of photographic paper. Shortly thereafter, it began rapidly expanding its sales force and concluded an agreement with the Rank organization in Britain to sell products outside the United States. By the end of 1957, the firm's yearly sales were $26 million and its staff had grown to 1,500.

In the late 1950s, Haloid-Xerox (its new name) continued to bring out successful non-xerographic products. One of these, the Copyflo 24, enlarged 35mm microfilm pictures of engineering drawings. But the main thrust was in xerography, where the firm now owned 126 patents. The main development target was the 914 office copier. This revolutionary machine cost millions more to create and market than was first anticipated, but it repaid that investment many times over.

The 914 was introduced for sale in February 1960. It was a big machine (650 pounds) that was leased to customers starting at $95 per month. It made six good quality copies per minute with a minimum of mess and effort. Compared to competitive machines with different technologies sold by 3M, Kodak, American Photocopying Equipment, and others, the 914 was a show stopper.

Business Week put Wilson and the 914 on the cover in September 1959. Nevertheless, when he predicted that this product could double the firm's sales to $60 million by 1965, some people thought he was mad. No one dreamed that actual revenues in 1965 would be $392.6 million or that the 914 would go on to be the most profitable product in the history of U.S. business.

The 1960s were just short of unbelievable for Xerox. The firm grew and grew, adding offices and plants and scores of excellent people who wanted to be associated with a winner. In 1963, the 813 "desktop" copier was introduced. In 1965, ahead of schedule, a model six times faster than the 914 was offered for sale (the Xerox 2400). Managing internal growth became an extraordinarily complex task. Executives were recruited from Ford (Archie McCardell and Jack Goldman), IBM (Joe Flavin and David Kearns), Standard Oil (Robert Haigh), and elsewhere. By the end of 1968, they were running a firm with revenues of $1.125 billion. Net income that year was $138 million—or about twenty times the firm's revenues when Joe Wilson became president.

*   *   *

Today, it is difficult to determine what kind of a culture Haloid had in its earliest years. One book by a long-term employee has anecdotes suggesting a tendency toward keeping costs down as well as a certain tenacity. There is also some evidence of a bias toward high quality products which were "valuable to their users," toward socially responsible behavior, and toward treating employees well.[7]

The culture at Haloid in the 1950s is clearer. Joe Wilson dominated the firm after World War II. His principles are said to have been "faith in people, concern for customers, and economic power through innovation, marketing, patents, and worldwide presence."[8] The concern for customers is a theme that emerges again and again in material describing the 1945–65 period.[9]

There is no question, however, that Xerox's culture underwent a significant transformation in the 1960s. By 1970, there were remnants of the previous values; the concern for trying to be a socially responsible employer still existed. But much else had changed. Managers had become arrogant. In 1968 Xerox purchased a small computer company named Scientific Data Systems for ninety times earnings and then attempted to challenge IBM directly, despite evidence that this strategy had been disastrous for others.[10] By this time, Xerox's concern for customers had diminished to the point where a pro-business administration in Washington began antitrust actions against the firm.

Whatever concern most managers had for stockholders and costs was also weakened. Little effort in engineering seems to have gone toward designing low-cost products.[11] The firm spent lavishly on buildings, good causes, and employee benefits instead.

Related to all this, Xerox became increasingly insular. Douglas Smith and Robert Alexander's highly critical book on the firm claims that "instead of measuring themselves against the needs of customers and the performance of competitors, Xerox's talented people competed among themselves in a race for personal aggrandizement."[12] A consultant to Xerox at the time put it this way: "Most of the decisions are made around issues of turf, career advancement, and those kinds of things."[13] The strongest evidence of insularity comes not from muck-raking journalists but from a 1971 book on the company by a long-term Xerox executive, *My Years with Xerox*. In its 239 pages, *My Years* never once mentions the potential threat of Japanese competition!

The culture at Xerox also became somewhat intolerant of initiatives and leadership from the ranks. Decision making was often centralized.[14] Experimentation was often discouraged, and error was not tolerated well. The person who ran the firm on a day-to-day basis was described by one of his colleagues as "a very, very, extremely bright individual. But he managed by the numbers. He wasn't a very good communicator."[15]

The consequences of all this were devastating. When a small task force examined Xerox's strategy in 1973 and 1974, their recommendations—some of them quite good—were apparently ignored.[16] When its Palo Alto Research Center invented the personal computer, executives decided not to exploit the opportunity.[17] When Canon, Minolta, Ricoh, and Sharp began introducing copier products in 1975, Xerox was very slow in responding; by 1980, the Japanese were selling copiers in the United States at a price below what it cost Xerox to make comparable models.[18] Overall, the firm failed to adapt to the changing conditions in the copier business, and as a result, its worldwide share of copier revenues fell from 82 percent in 1976 to 41 percent in 1982.[19] It also failed completely to adapt to the requirements of the computer industry; to date, its multi-billion dollar effort has not earned the firm one cent of profit in computer sales.

More than a few observers believe that if the culture that caused this destruction had not been significantly changed in the 1980s, Xerox may actually have gone bankrupt.

*   *   *

Xerox may be an extreme case, but less extreme examples are not uncommon among today's large firms.[20] There appear to be many big companies with cultures that are either somewhat arrogant, inward looking, or stifling of initiative, and as a result, help undermine long-term economic performance.

But why? We think the answer lies in the scenario shown in exhibit 6.3. To survive over a significant period and become a major player in an industry requires some considerable amount of success. And this very success, in a sense, poisons the culture.

But then why don't all large firms have problem cultures? The Hewlett-Packard case suggests one answer: founders create a performance-enhancing culture early in a firm's life, then they (and their successors) explicitly reinforce (verbally and in writing) the adaptive core of that culture when it comes under assault from too much success. They behave humbly themselves, displayed great concern for all the firm's constituencies, and encouraged competent leadership throughout their hierarchies. The ten causes discussed in the next chapter offer a second answer to the question. There we will see very capable leaders and their associates in mature firms actually change unhealthy cultures to make them more performance enhancing.

What are the consequences when a large number of big firms have problem cultures? Exhibit 6.4 offers some answers. The twelve firms in our second study that had performance-enhancing cultures increased their revenues four times as much between 1977 and 1988 as did the twenty firms from our third study that had problem cultures. The twelve increased the number of people they employed by eight times as much and their stock price by 12 times as much. They raised their net incomes, and hence the taxes they paid, by over 700 percent versus no increase for the twenty. No matter how one looks at the issue, the economic and social consequences of unhealthy cultures loom large.

How difficult is it to transform problem cultures into ones that enhance long-term economic performance? If the experiences of the twenty firms discussed in this chapter are representative the answer is: most difficult.[21] Over the last ten to

EXHIBIT 6.4

THE ECONOMICS AND SOCIAL COSTS OF LOW-PERFORMANCE CULTURES
(1977–1988)

	Average for Twelve Firms with Performance-Enhancing Cultures (%)	Average for Twenty Firms without Performance-Enhancing Cultures (%)
Revenue Growth	682	166
Employment Growth	282	36
Stock Price Growth	901	74
Tax Base (Net Income) Growth	756	1

twenty years, virtually all of these companies have had some managers either express the need for change or try to effect that change. Yet, only a few of these firms have made significant progress toward creating more performance-enhancing cultures, and that progress has come very slowly.

Cultures that lack adaptive values at their core tend to behave like mattresses or sofas with inner springs; it is possible to change the shape of a part of these structures with the application of sufficient force, but as soon as the force is removed or lessened the original shape often returns. At least four fundamental characteristics of culture appear to be responsible for this behavior: (1) interdependence between and within the levels of culture (values, behavior/practices), (2) interdependence between culture and the power structure in an organization, (3) the usual culture-perpetuating mechanisms, and (4) the strong connection between values and human emotions. Because of the interdependence between values and behavior, executives sometimes make needed changes in the policies or formal structures or architecture and achieve some limited change in behavior patterns. But because some values that are inconsistent with those behaviors remain unchanged, forces build to reinstate old practices—forces that over a period of time invariably grow powerful enough to succeed.[22] Because culture is interdependent and usually helps support the power structure in a firm, that power structure usually fights change that might threaten its privileges. The resistance is subtle and covert—and it is often successful.[23] Because of perpetuating mechanisms, executives sometimes successfully change not only the behaviors but even some of the values of a small subgroup of their managers only to find that those changes are eroded over time by the actions of the rest of the group. What is communicated, praised, penalized, and supported by the old majority slowly undermines the new subgroup culture. Because culture touches human values, when someone tries to change deeply held values, people often react emotionally. Fearing the pain of loss, they cling to the old and familiar.

In an increasingly competitive world, the capacity to introduce new strategies and practices is a necessity. In many firms, the anchor on such change is cultural. Executives successfully alter formal structures, announce new strategies, hire new executives, buy new information technology, and build new plants or headquarters, but still don't produce needed behavioral changes because of the resistant culture. Indeed, changing problem cultures is so difficult that some observers have concluded that it is virtually impossible. But as we will see next, that appears not to be true.

III

The Change Question:

HOW CAN CORPORATE CULTURES BE PURPOSEFULLY CHANGED TO MAKE THEM MORE PERFORMANCE ENHANCING?

7

PEOPLE WHO CREATE SUCCESSFUL CHANGE

The first books on corporate culture either ignored the issue of change or presented relatively simplistic formulas for making major changes.[1] The more recent literature is much more pessimistic on this topic and quite critical of earlier formulas. Alan Wilkins reflects the feelings of many academics when he says "Culture has been trivialized because so many have written about 'managing culture,' 'managing myths,' or 'creating meaning' without serious attention to just how difficult it is to manipulate these complex social processes."[2] He backs up this assertion with evidence that in twenty-two cases of attempted "cultural change," even the managers themselves (who tended to declare victory based on the slimmest of evidence) admitted they had failed in sixteen of the situations.[3]

We have already described instances of incremental cultural change in firms with adaptive cultures (Chapters 4 and 5). Here we focus on major change, particularly in large organizations. We have identified and studied ten such cases:[4] American Express's Travel Related Services, Bankers Trust, British Airways, ConAgra, First Chicago, General Electric, Nissan, ICI, SAS, and Xerox.[5] In all ten situations, most observers inside and outside these firms agree that a cultural change of some significance had taken place sometime in the last fifteen years. In all these cases, the corporate cultures seem to have grown to look more, although not completely, like those described in Chapter 5—with core values that stressed customers, other key constituencies, and leadership at multiple levels in the hierarchy, and with behavior patterns that fit the real needs of the business environment. And in all ten situations, these changes were accompanied by some performance improvements that seem at least partially related to the new cultures. Exhibit 7.1 describes the performance improvements.

These ten cases help to explain both why major cultural change appears to be rare and yet how it is feasible. In this chapter we will look at who led the change effort in these stories. In the next, we will discuss *how* they did so.

*   *   *

The single most visible factor that distinguishes major cultural changes that succeed from those that fail is competent leadership at the top.[6] In all ten of the cases we studied, major change began after an individual who already had a track record for leadership was appointed to head an organization. Each of these individuals had previously shown the capacity to do more than manage well;[7] as exhibit 7.2 shows, they knew how to produce change and were willing to do just that. In their new jobs, they did this again, albeit on a grander scale. Each new leader created a team that established a new vision and set of strategies for achieving that vision. Each new leader succeeded in persuading important groups and individuals in the firm to commit themselves to that new direction and then energized the personnel sufficiently to make it happen, despite all the obstacles.[8] Ultimately, hundreds (or even thousands) of people helped make all the changes in strategies, products, structures, policies, personnel, and (eventually) culture. But often, just one or two people seem to have been essential in getting the process started.

At Bankers Trust, Alfred Brittain III and Charlie Sanford formed a team that helped change the corporate culture from a traditional commercial bank, highly valuing a measured pace of decision making, to a more transaction-oriented global merchant

EXHIBIT 7.1

TEN CASES OF MAJOR CULTURAL CHANGE

COMPANY	Period of Cultural Change	Long-Term Economic Performance
Bankers Trust	1977–1985	Annual growth in return on assets rose from − 8.71% in 1967–1976 to + 14.09% in 1977–1988
British Airways	1982–1985	Firm turned around from losses of £ 520 million in 1977–1982 to profits of £ 1,059 million in 1984–1989
ConAgra	1974–1978	Stock grew in value fiftyfold over fourteen years
First Chicago	Since 1981	Profits grew from $200 million in 1979–80 to nearly $900 million in 1988–89. This trend is ongoing
General Electric	Since 1980	Market value has grown from $12 billion to $60 billion in ten years. This trend is ongoing
ICI	1982–1987	Net income rose 500% from 1982 to 1987
Nissan	Since 1985	After a fifteen-year decline, domestic market share rose in 1988–89. Net income rose from $165 million in 1987 to $939 million in 1990. This trend is ongoing
SAS	1980–1983	Net income grew from SKr 450 million in 1974–1981 to SKr 12 billion in 1982–1989
American Express TRS	1978–1983	Profits have risen 18% annually for a decade despite an onslaught of new competition
Xerox	1983–1989	Return on assets rose from 5% to 12.4% and revenue from $8.5 billion to $17.5 billion between 1983 and 1989. Copier market share rose from 8.6% in the early 1980s to 16% in 1991. In 1991 Xerox won the Malcolm Baldrige National Quality Award

EXHIBIT 7.2

THE EARLY TRACK RECORDS OF ELEVEN INDIVIDUALS WHO
SUCCESSFULLY LED MAJOR CULTURAL CHANGE EFFORTS

Jan Carlzon	Turned around two SAS subsidiaries: Vingresor (1974–1978) and Linjeflyg (1978–1980)
Lou Gerstner	Developed a business practice at McKinsey (in the 1970s) at an unusually young age
Mike Harper	At Pillsbury, led effort to develop and install modern management and control systems in the plants, revitalized R & D, and helped turn around their poultry business
Sir John Harvey-Jones	Led the effort to solve huge labor relations problems at ICI's Petrochemicals business (at Wilton)
David Kearns	In the late 1970s, turned around Xerox management's complacent attitude about the seriousness of the Japanese threat
Lord King	Founded Ferrybridge Industries in 1945 (later named Pollard Bell and Roller Bearing Co.) and built it into a successful business. Successfully restructured Babcock International in the 1970s
Yutaka Kume	Was one of the leaders of an effort to modernize Nissan manufacturing facilities in the 1970s
Sir Colin Marshall	Helped develop Avis operations in Europe and around the world
Charlie Sanford	Built the bond trading operations at Bankers Trust into a much bigger and more profitable business
Barry Sullivan	Developed a reputation as a leader at Chase Manhattan Bank
Jack Welch	Helped build GE's plastics business into a major and very profitable division

banking organization, emphasizing fast reactions, state-of-the-art communications, sophisticated controls, and profits. In 1977, Brittain and Sanford sold off Bankers Trust's retail banking and credit card operations; this set the stage for a second round of planning in 1981 and 1982 that led to the creation of a worldwide merchant bank. The best people available were recruited at market rates, regardless of title. Senior managers began calling each other "partner," as is the custom in Bankers Trust's new investment banking competitors, and these "partners" fostered a similar entrepreneurial culture at lower levels in the organization. As a result of all of the changes, the growth rate of Bankers Trust's return on assets soared to an average of 14.1 percent for the years 1977 through 1988 compared to a minus 8.7 percent average for the comparable period ten years earlier.

At British Airways, leadership also came from two people at the top: Lord King and Sir Colin Marshall. King became chairman at BA in 1981. Marshall became CEO in 1983. With their assistance, the BA culture eventually became more customer focused, somewhat more sensitive to cost, productivity, and profits, and more encouraging of initiative from employees. Net income grew from a loss of £520 million in the period 1977–1982 to a profit of £1,059 million in 1984–1989.[9]

At ConAgra, the extraordinary leadership started with Mike Harper, who became CEO of the Omaha-based food company in 1976. Within a few years, a new culture began to take hold, one that emphasized results for shareholders through satisfying customer needs, one that placed a huge premium on competent leadership at the business unit level, and one that was committed to creating an environment attractive to highly capable people. Those familiar with ConAgra say the new culture has unquestionably helped contribute to the firm's incredible results over the past fourteen years: a tenfold increase in net income and a fiftyfold increase in stock value.[10]

At First Chicago, the new leader was Barry Sullivan, appointed chairman in 1980. Under Sullivan, First Chicago has slowly risen from the ashes, developing a stronger and healthier culture to replace the social chaos created by a series of financial disasters in the late 1970s. Net income increased from less than $200 million in 1979–80 to nearly $900 million in 1988–89.

At General Electric, the leader is Jack Welch. Since becoming chairman in 1981, Welch has helped change GE's business mix and corporate culture in some ways that are truly dramatic. The GE of 1990 is considerably less bureaucratic and more supportive of leadership initiatives throughout the firm; there are fewer layers, fewer control-oriented staff, and fewer sterile business reviews. The company is more committed to productivity growth and excellence for shareholders. It is also more externally focused on customers and competition globally. Under Welch, GE's net income has risen thus far from $1.5 billion to more than $4.0 billion, and its market value has gone from $12 billion to over $60 billion.[11]

At ICI, the new chairman in 1982 was Sir John Harvey-Jones. Like Welch, he changed some of ICI's businesses and significantly affected its culture. Before Harvey-Jones, ICI was a highly conservative, centralized, and bureaucratic chemical company. After Harvey-Jones, the corporate culture was less conservative, more decentralized, and more encouraging of leadership from the businesses. It was also more externally focused on markets and customers. The economic payoff was impressive: net income during Harvey-Jones's five-year chairmanship rose over 500 percent. Most observers would credit a significant part of that increase to cultural changes.[12]

At Nissan, major change began when Yutaka Kume was made president in 1985. Subsequently, Nissan's inward-looking, bureaucratic culture has become more focused on customers, on making money, and on empowering people lower in the organization. At least partially as a result of this, the firm's profits increased from just under $165 million in 1987 to nearly $940 million in 1990.[13]

At SAS, the new culture emerged after Jan Carlzon became CEO in 1981. That culture placed a higher premium on serving targeted groups of customers, was more supportive of leadership up and down the hierarchy, was somewhat more concerned with making a profit, and paid a great deal of attention to employees. Under Carlzon, profits soared from a total of SKr 450 million in the period 1974–1981 to SKr 12 billion in 1982–1989.[14]

At the Travel Related Services (TRS) unit of American Express, the leader was Lou Gerstner. In 1978, he took over TRS and helped change it into an organization that could more effectively deal with an onslaught of new competition. Under Gerstner and his team, TRS's culture became increasingly entrepreneurial, focused on segmented customer groups, concerned about productivity, and appreciative of highly talented employees. The economic payoff from good leadership, good business strategies, and then a better culture was dramatic: despite more competition in a business many people defined as mature, TRS's net income grew for a decade at an annual rate of about 18 percent per year.[15]

At Xerox, cultural change has come about largely as a result of the leadership of David Kearns. When Kearns became chairman in 1983, the culture was a huge obstacle to change. Under Kearns, that culture did change: especially regarding a heightened commitment to quality products to satisfy customer needs. Without that shift, Xerox's core copier business probably would have been bankrupt by now as a result of extremely tough Japanese competition.[16]

Competition is a central theme going through all these cases. Effective leaders changed strategies and cultures to make their firms more competitive despite the natural tendency of cultures to resist change, despite the large size and mature environments found in most of these cases, despite everything. And in the process, these individuals demonstrated how closely interrelated are five topics of great interest in managerial circles today: competition, leadership, change, strategy, and culture.

*   *   *

It is interesting to look at the backgrounds of the eleven people whose leadership is most closely linked to these cases of major cultural change. In addition to the leadership theme, one other pattern is striking. All eleven of these executives either came into their positions from outside their firms, came to their firms after an early career somewhere else, "grew up" outside the core of their companies, or were unconventional in some other way (see exhibit 7.3). To some substantial degree, they all brought with them an "outsider" perspective, that broader view and greater emotional detachment that is so uncharacteristic of people that have been thoroughly acculturated in an organization. Insofar that each of these people had to see that their firms needed drastic change, see what the alternatives were, and then have the strength to go against the established order, one cannot help but wonder if that "outsider" perspective might not be an essential ingredient in these stories.[17]

One whom we've listed as an unconventional insider, Char-

EXHIBIT 7.3

THE CAREER PATHS OF ELEVEN INDIVIDUALS WHOSE LEADERSHIP HELPED PRODUCE MAJOR CULTURAL CHANGE

Jan Carlzon	Unconventional Insider	Grew up in SAS, but not in the core business
Lou Gerstner	Outsider	Came to TRS in 1978 as executive vice president. Grew up in McKinsey, where his main client was TRS
Mike Harper	Outsider	Came to ConAgra in 1974 as executive vice president. Grew up in Pillsbury
Sir John Harvey-Jones	Insider/ Outsider	Came to ICI at age 33 after abandoning a career in the Royal Navy. Unlike the rest of top management, not a chemist
David Kearns	Insider/ Outsider	Came to Xerox at age 42 after a successful career at IBM
Lord King	Outsider	Came to British Airways as chairman in 1981
Yutaka Kume	Unconventional Insider	Grew up at Nissan, but with a career path very different from his predecessors
Sir Colin Marshall	Outsider	Became CEO at British Airways in 1983. Came from Sears Holdings
Charlie Sanford	Unconventional Insider	Grew up at Bankers Trust, but not in the core business. Came to the bank with an education quite different from the norm in senior management
Barry Sullivan	Outsider	Came to First Chicago in 1980 as chairman. Grew up in Chase Manhattan Bank
Jack Welch	Unconventional Insider	Grew up in GE's plastics business, a newer and non-mainline business for GE

lie Sanford, illustrates what we mean quite well. In a firm full of Yale graduates, Sanford came to Bankers Trust in 1963 from the University of Georgia and Wharton Business School. His career took off after he ran the Bank's fledgling bond trading operation, a distinctly nontraditional banking experience for the early 1970s. Sanford is said to be an avid reader and debater of subjects as diverse as theology, baroque art, and quantum mechanics. He even brews his own beer. If that doesn't set him apart from his more traditional counterparts at other banks, he is described by one colleague as having a "constitutional inability to be second-best at anything."[18] An insight into how he sees his function at Bankers Trust is provided by one of his own comments: "There's a deliberate policy here to create a level of anxiety. Winners usually play like they're one touchdown behind."[19]

But there is a dilemma here made clear by a second pattern (shown in exhibit 7.4). The larger the organization, the more likely it is that the new leader has an insider background, with its accompanying credibility, relationships, and power base. The new leaders at the four largest companies (GE, Nissan, ICI, Xerox) in our sample include no complete outsiders. The pure outsiders are found in four of the five smallest firms. The most logical inference is that without insider resources, which can be accumulated quickly in a small organization but not in a large one, a CEO may be able to see what is needed, but be unable to implement that vision.[20]

Taken together, these three characteristics—effective leader, outsider's perspective, and insider's resources—are not found in many people, at least today. Studies have shown that, at best, organizations produce some individuals with strong insider resources.[21] Rarely do they develop strong leaders[22] or executives with an outsider's perspective.[23] Perhaps this is one reason why major cultural change is relatively rare nowadays, despite the apparent need for such change in a significant number of organizations.

These patterns may also help further explain why strategically appropriate but unadaptive cultures do not perform better over the long term. In a changing business environment, those cultures will regularly need a major change every five to twenty-five years depending upon how fast events move. But that change will probably not occur unless a relatively rare com-

EXHIBIT 7.4

THE RELATIONSHIP OF SIZE OF FIRM TO THE BACKGROUND
OF THE CENTRAL FIGURES IN TEN CASES OF MAJOR
CULTURAL CHANGE

Size of Organization	Firm	Background of Change Agent
Very Large	General Electric	Unconventional Insider
	ICI	Insider/Outsider
	Nissan	Unconventional Insider
	Xerox	Insider/Outsider
Large	Bankers Trust	Unconventional Insider
	First Chicago	Outsider
	American Express TRS	Outsider
	British Air	Outsider
Medium	SAS	Unconventional Insider
	ConAgra	Outsider

modity is found—a strong leader with insider resources and an
outsider perspective. Some firms, some of the time, might find
such a person. But it seems likely that most firms, most of the
time, will not.

*   *   *

Leadership from one or two people at the very top of an organization seems to be an absolutely essential ingredient when
major cultural change occurs. But why? Why can't such change
be created in a more bottom-up process, with the initiative coming from middle- or lower-level management?

There are probably two basic reasons why none of our cases
of major change can be characterized as bottom-up. The first is
related to the sheer difficulty of changing cultures—to overcoming their spring back resistance quality. Great power is required, and that power normally resides only at the top of

hierarchies. The second reason relates to interdependence inside organizations, which can make it difficult to change anything a great deal without changing everything. Usually the only people in a position to initiate change of that scope are those on top.

Lower- and middle-level managers are not, however, irrelevant in these stories. Ultimately, it is their actions that produce the changes. And in a number of the cases we studied, their activities helped the new senior-level leader to obtain the top position by giving needed backing to his candidacy. They also often provided him with critical help during his first twelve to twenty-four months; they created pockets of support inside the organization for his activities when support was most badly needed. The importance of these actions should not be underestimated.

8

LEADERS IN ACTION

In the ten cases of major cultural change that we studied, the executives leading these efforts all got off to a relatively fast start after being appointed CEO, COO, or head of a business.[1] These individuals appear to have developed a strong belief in the need for change before their appointments. In some cases, they also had a relatively clear vision of the kinds of changes that were needed. Although it is difficult to validate, it would appear that in many (possibly all) cases these people were asked to run their organizations because they had those beliefs and visions.

In varying degrees, each of these leaders seems to have begun his new job by trying to create an atmosphere of perceived "crisis." This was never easy. In only three of the ten cases were losses reported before these individuals took charge (see exhibit 8.1), and segments of even those three companies still did not believe that a crisis was at hand. In at least two situations, GE and American Express TRS, most employees believed that their firms were doing exceptionally well and hence needed little or no change.[2]

To create a perceived need for change, these leaders communicated widely the facts that pointed to a crisis or potential

EXHIBIT 8.1

THE DEGREE OF "CRISIS" BEFORE THE CHANGE EFFORT WAS
INSTITUTED

Firm	Organization-wide losses reported before change effort was instituted
American Express TRS	None
Bankers Trust	None
British Airways	Significant losses in 1981 (7% of revenues)
ConAgra	Moderate loss reported in 1974 (3% of revenues)
First Chicago	None
General Electric	None
ICI	None
Nissan	None
SAS	Small loss reported in 1980 (2% of revenues)
Xerox	None

crisis.[3] When convincing data was not available, they created
new measurement systems to obtain it. Often they also hired
consultants and appointed task forces (or encouraged others to
do so) to gather and communicate that kind of information. Although no one readily admits doing so, in a few cases they clearly
manufactured the data they needed by, for example, permitting
or engineering a sufficiently convincing loss in income for a quarter or a year.

At the same time, these leaders developed or clarified their
visions of what changes were needed. Typically, this was done
by challenging the status quo with very basic questions. Are we
meeting customers' needs better than the competition? If not,
why not? Are we producing our goods and services as efficiently
as possible? To address these issues, they drew on a broad range
of information—from all parts of the business, from people out-

side the organization (customers, consultants, suppliers), and from managers at the lowest levels in their firms.[4] In virtually all ten cases, the degree to which the leaders challenged the status quo and the breadth of information they marshalled to address key issues far exceeded what was done by their predecessors.

After perceiving some minimum readiness on the part of their managers, the leaders then began communicating their visions of what changes were necessary. These visions always carried some general message about key constituencies, especially customers, and about leadership or impediments to leadership (e.g., excessive bureaucracy). Also included was information about more specific strategies and practices that were seen as needed to deal with the current business climate or competitive situation.

Visions and strategies were communicated with words—spoken simply, directly, and often—and with deeds. In some cases (British Airways, Nissan, SAS, Xerox), these top managers spent far more time communicating with their employees than their predecessors had. In most cases, they encouraged people to engage in a dialogue with them, not allowing the communication to flow in one direction only. In almost all cases, the leaders became living embodiments of the cultures they desired. The values and practices they wanted infused into their firms were usually on display in their daily behavior: in the questions they asked at meetings, in how they spent their time, in the decisions they made. These actions seem to have given critical credibility to their words. The behavior made it clear to others that their speeches were serious. And successes, which seemed to result from that behavior, made it clear that the speeches were sensible.[5]

Visions were also communicated to appeal to the values of other executives and managers. In combination with a non-micromanagement style, a lot of cheerleading, and recognition for initiative, the leaders were able to motivate many other individuals to behave like them.[6] They successfully encouraged dozens, hundreds, or in very large situations, even thousands of managers to develop and implement new strategies and practices for their specific domains of responsibility. Sometimes this was easy because the managers were either unconventional or insider/outsiders themselves and had already been trying to in-

EXHIBIT 8.2

CHANGES IN EXECUTIVE BEHAVIOR THAT USUALLY
ACCOMPANY AND HELP CREATE THE EMERGENCE OF MORE
ADAPTIVE/PERFORMANCE-ENHANCING CULTURES

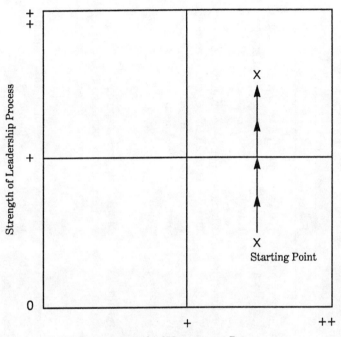

Strength of Management Process

troduce change. In other cases, this was very difficult, because
the managers clung tightly to the old culture. But overall, these
leaders succeeded in motivating enough other people that an
increasingly strong leadership process was developed throughout their organizations.

Winning over some of the more respected long service managers was usually an important part of these stories. These
managers then became role models for other long-term employees. Their ability to change and play a useful leadership role
signaled that others could also.

The establishment of a strong leadership process, not to
replace, but to supplement a management process, is an absolutely essential part of all of these stories of major cultural
change (see exhibit 8.2). Unlike even the very best management
process (see exhibit 8.3), leadership has as its primary function

EXHIBIT 8.3

THE DIFFERENCE BETWEEN MANAGEMENT AND LEADERSHIP

Management	Leadership
Planning and Budgeting—establishing detailed steps and timetables for achieving needed results, and then allocating the resources necessary to make that happen	Establishing direction—developing a vision of the future, often the distant future, and strategies for producing the changes needed to achieve that vision
Organizing and Staffing—establishing some structure for accomplishing plan requirements, staffing that structure with individuals, delegating responsibility and authority for carrying out the plan, providing policies and procedures to help guide people, and creating methods or systems to monitor implementation	Aligning People—communicating the direction by words and deeds to all those whose cooperation may be needed so as to influence the creation of teams and coalitions that understand the vision and strategies, and accept their validity
Controlling and Problem Solving—monitoring results vs. plan in some detail, identifying deviations, and then planning and organizing to solve these problems	Motivating and Inspiring—energizing people to overcome major political, bureaucratic, and resource barriers to change by satisfying very basic, but often unfulfilled, human needs
Produces a degree of predictability and order, and has the potential of consistently producing key results expected by various stakeholders (e.g., for customers, always being on time; for stockholders, being on budget)	Produces change, often to a dramatic degree, and has the potential of producing extremely useful change (e.g., new products that customers want, new approaches to labor relations that help make a firm more competitive)

Source: John P. Kotter, *A Force for Change: How Leadership Differs from Management*, p. 6.

the production of change. Without leadership, purposeful change of any magnitude is almost impossible.

*   *   *

In the ten successful cases of cultural change that we studied, hundreds or thousands of initiatives were required to implement the new visions and the new strategies, initiatives that usually focused more on behavior than on values.[7] People reorganized, often cutting levels and decentralizing responsibility to put managers close to customers and to make employees more accountable for profits. They endorsed activities proposed by others that would naturally give more responsibility to lower-level managers, or push people to talk to customers, or encourage people to learn about superior employee relations practices at other firms. They replaced managers with individuals whose values were more consistent with the cultures they desired—in diversified firms, often drawing those managers from the business units that already had the healthiest and most adaptive cultures. Even more fundamental, they changed the criteria used in selection and promotion decisions (see exhibit 8.4). Overall, hundreds of individuals initiated thousands of actions,[8] all working within some general framework provided by more senior level leaders.

In choosing among the opportunities that were available, these leaders looked for some quick but sustainable successes. Although they seemed very aware of the long time required for cultural change and displayed unusual persistence and patience, they were also impatient to create some successes that would give their efforts credibility. They wasted little time and energy on people or products or plants that seemed to have little long-term potential. As a result, in nine of the ten cases we studied, the leaders were able to demonstrate substantial positive results within their first two years (see exhibit 8.5). By creating systems that tracked nonfinancial data (on product quality, for example), they were also sometimes able to demonstrate credible progress in even less time.

The importance of results cannot be overstated. These new cultures grew in a cycle that was driven by successful results. At first, only a small number of like-minded people embraced the new strategies, practices, and values. Their actions produced positive results that not only reinforced new behavior and values in the original group but also attracted others.[9] This

EXHIBIT 8.4

INSTITUTIONALIZING IN A CULTURE A NEW VISION AND A NEW SET OF BUSINESS STRATEGIES

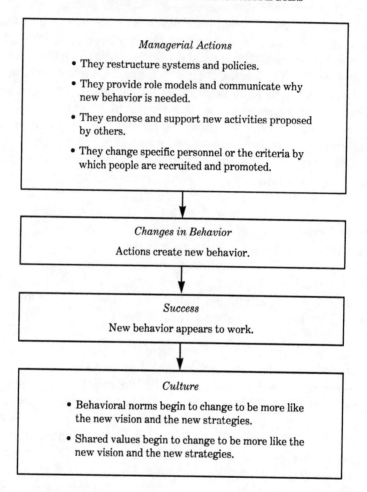

Managerial Actions

- They restructure systems and policies.
- They provide role models and communicate why new behavior is needed.
- They endorse and support new activities proposed by others.
- They change specific personnel or the criteria by which people are recruited and promoted.

Changes in Behavior

Actions create new behavior.

Success

New behavior appears to work.

Culture

- Behavioral norms begin to change to be more like the new vision and the new strategies.
- Shared values begin to change to be more like the new vision and the new strategies.

larger group then acted, produced some positive results, and grew. The cycle continued.

In all the cases of major cultural change that required more than a few years, the momentum produced by this cycle was lost at least once. Sometimes this was the result of a business failure that people associated with the cultural change. Sometimes this was simply due to growing forces of resistance or general exhaus-

EXHIBIT 8.5

EARLY SUCCESS IN CHANGE EFFORTS

Firm	Results within First Two Years
American Express TRS	Profits up despite more competition
Bankers Trust	Profits up substantially
British Airways	Losses stopped. Firm profitable again
ConAgra	Losses stopped. Firm profitable again
First Chicago	Profits up substantially
General Electric	Profits up. Stock price doubled
ICI	Profits up substantially
Nissan	Little visible improvement
SAS	Losses stopped. Firm profitable again
Xerox	Return on assets up substantially

tion in the management ranks. In all these instances, stopping the change would have been easy and welcomed. Nevertheless, that rarely happened. Instead, the executive leaders stepped up the level of activities aimed at change, sometimes taking charge directly—at least until momentum was regained.

Taken together, these themes help explain why major cultural change does not happen more often in large organizations. It requires an effective leader on top. He or she must have both an outsider's openness to new ideas and an insider's power base. This leader must create a perceived need for change even if most people believe all is well. He must create and communicate effectively a new vision and set of strategies, and then behave accordingly on a daily basis. He must motivate an increasingly large group of people to help with this leadership effort. These people must find hundreds or thousands of opportunities to influence behavior. And the resulting actions on the part of a growing group of people must produce positive results; if they do not, the whole effort loses critical credibility.

*   *   *

The case of First Chicago demonstrates most of these themes and introduces yet another characteristic of any effort to bring about major cultural change: the amount of time required.[10]

First Chicago was chartered in 1863 and grew very successfully in the midwestern United States. By 1958 it had surpassed dozens of older eastern banks to become the seventh largest organization of its kind in the country. It had a good reputation and a good relationship with its employees. Its culture was fairly strong, emphasizing a commitment to customers, a strong credit process, a belief in itself as a first-class institution, a focus on corporate lending, and the use of specialized groups to look at different industries.

First Chicago opened an office in London in 1959 and expanded to Japan in 1962. By the late 1960s a much more aggressive and expansive culture began to take hold, led by Gaylord Freeman, who served as chairman from 1969 to 1975. The bank opened more and more foreign offices, offered Harvard MBAs fast-track careers, and became more transaction/deal oriented. It moved away from its geographical roots and from traditional credit-oriented banking. The initial results of these changes were very impressive; profits more than doubled between 1970 and 1975. But then the bank went into a tailspin.

In retrospect, it's easy to see that First Chicago expanded far beyond its capabilities and resources. The problems created by overexpansion were aggravated and multiplied by the 1974 recession and a politicized three-way race to replace Freeman as chairman.

Robert Aboud won that race. Using an autocratic style, he began to rein in the institution, restricting growth, cutting employees, and instituting rigid internal controls. Fast-track MBAs began to leave, morale dropped, and problem loans became more frequent. Conflict and chaos threatened to become the norm.

In 1980, with net income down 60 percent from 1975 levels, the top three officers of the bank resigned, and the board brought in Barry Sullivan from Chase to be CEO. By then, many observers say, the bank was "on its knees," its traditional culture having been "shattered."

Raised in the Bronx and educated by Jesuit priests, Sullivan was both an excellent student and basketball player. He eventually attended business school at the University of Chicago and ended up at Chase, where he did exceptionally well and developed, according to one magazine article, "a cult following." A former Chase official, now at Mellon, says, "He was a real leader, a very exciting guy."[11]

In his first six months at First Chicago, Sullivan brought in fourteen key executives from outside the bank. He gave them and others profit-center responsibility and urged them to provide leadership to their businesses. He then began to try to create an overall strategy for the bank and a corporate culture that would allow those leadership initiatives to work together for the good of the institution.

The strategy Sullivan and his new team started creating emphasized a commitment to customers, a strong credit process (to support profitability), teamwork, and an increasingly domestic and regional focus. In support of this new focus, they bought Bankers Trust's credit card business in 1982 and a Chicago "middle market" bank, named American National, in 1984.

Performance began to improve soon after Sullivan arrived and continued to improve as his new organization and culture began to take hold. Profits in 1981 were $118 million, nearly double 1980 levels. 1982 net income was $136 million. 1983 net income grew to $183 million. As a result, a happy Sullivan declared publicly that First Chicago had "turned around." It did look that way in early 1984.

In October of 1984, the bank reported a quarterly loss of $71.8 million, mostly related to bad real estate loans. These results were unexpected and unprecedented; the bank had never in its entire history reported a loss before. A few months later, still another loss was recorded, this time because of a Brazilian acquisition. It was a terrible period for Sullivan and his supporters. The fragile culture they had created started to collapse, with bickering and second-guessing among the management.

Instead of retreating, Sullivan accepted responsibility for those bad results and charged forward even more aggressively. He led efforts by a group of his managers to overhaul the credit system completely. His executive team cleaned up the loan portfolio, cut back international operations even more, and bought two small Illinois banking groups. To further reinforce the emphasis on customer service and teamwork, they instituted a daily meeting of top managers in the corporate bank to discuss customers and their problems. They also redesigned compensation and evaluation processes to focus more on overall results, not just individual performance.

These efforts paid off. The new culture rebounded and took on additional strength, both creating and being created by impressive bottom line results: 1986 net income was more than triple 1984 levels, $270 million versus $86 million.

Then in 1987, along with many other large U.S. banks, First Chicago was forced to increase its reserves for third world loan losses, resulting in a net loss for the year of half a billion dollars. Because everyone recognized that this was unrelated to the basic operation of the bank, another crisis did not develop. Nevertheless, the 1987 loss, in combination with the newer and more adaptive culture, seems to have spurred even more changes. At this juncture, Sullivan's executives jettisoned more international business, acquired more retail banking operations in Chicago and its suburbs, and bought another large addition to the credit card business. Sullivan himself began working harder to create a team of managers at the top of the organization that really shared key values and styles—efforts which resulted in more turnover.

1988 results were excellent; net income rose to $513 million, six times the 1984 figure. By late that year, some observers were finally saying that the bank had rebounded. A Salomon Brothers research report published in February 1989 had the following title: "First Chicago Corporation—A Dominant Force in the Midwest."

*   *   *

It took Barry Sullivan and his managers nine years to institute a new culture at First Chicago, and yet best evidence in 1991 suggests that the culture is still fragile and problematic. Jack Welch spent most of the 1980s leading the cultural-change effort at GE and predicted it would require another decade to finish the job. David Kearns spent seven or eight years helping to change some aspects of Xerox's culture, and critics of the firm say there is much more still to be done.

The evidence clearly says that major cultural change does not happen easily or quickly, especially in large organizations (see exhibit 8.6).[12] Even the incremental changes made in (and by) the performance-enhancing culture at Hewlett-Packard sometimes came slowly and with great effort. In big organiza-

EXHIBIT 8.6

TIME REQUIRED FOR CULTURAL CHANGE

Firm	Size When Change Initiated	Length of Major Cultural Change Effort
General Electric	Very Large	10 years and continuing
ICI		6 years
Nissan		6 years and continuing
Xerox		7 years
Bankers Trust	Large	8 years
First Chicago		10 years
American Express TRS		6 years
British Airways		4 years
SAS	Medium	4 years
ConAgra		4 years

tions, even with excellent leadership at the top, major change requires many initiatives from many people,[13] and that simply requires time, often lots of it. Perhaps this is why good results along the way are so important. They give credibility to those providing leadership and to the process itself. And they help people to be patient (see exhibit 8.7).

Because of the difficulty, executives appear to fail often in their efforts to make a big cultural change. Many more don't seem to even try. As a result, some managers have probably never seen a successful case of significant change of this kind, at least in a firm of any size. And they may logically wonder if it is really possible. It is, and the case of ICI is a good example.

EXHIBIT 8.7

THE CREATION OF A PERFORMANCE-ENHANCING CULTURE

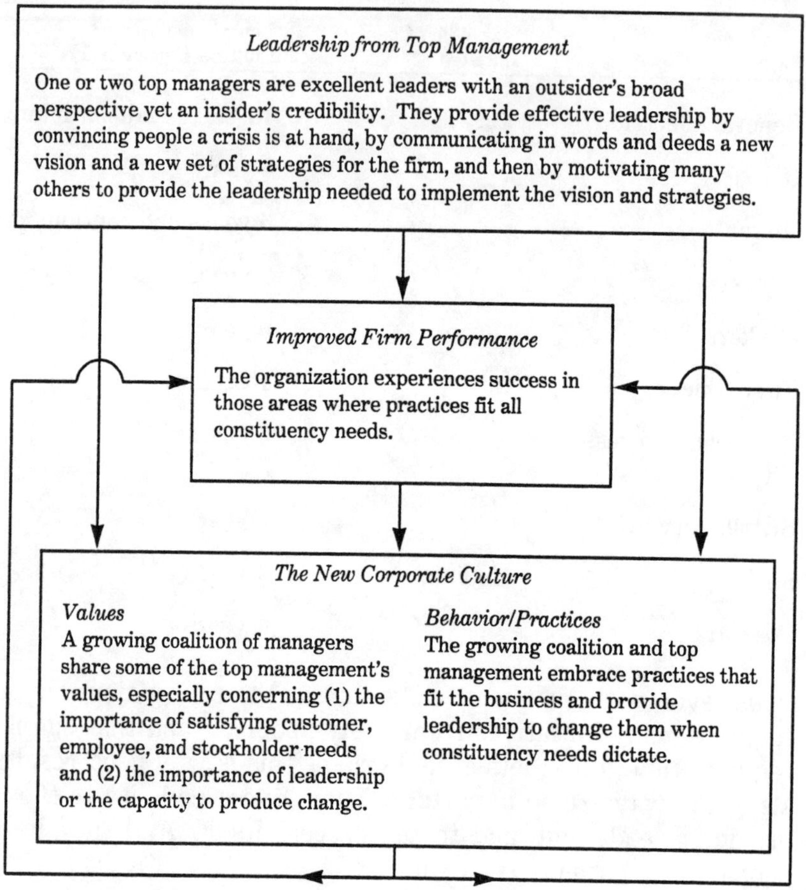

Leadership from Top Management

One or two top managers are excellent leaders with an outsider's broad perspective yet an insider's credibility. They provide effective leadership by convincing people a crisis is at hand, by communicating in words and deeds a new vision and a new set of strategies for the firm, and then by motivating many others to provide the leadership needed to implement the vision and strategies.

Improved Firm Performance

The organization experiences success in those areas where practices fit all constituency needs.

The New Corporate Culture

Values
A growing coalition of managers share some of the top management's values, especially concerning (1) the importance of satisfying customer, employee, and stockholder needs and (2) the importance of leadership or the capacity to produce change.

Behavior/Practices
The growing coalition and top management embrace practices that fit the business and provide leadership to change them when constituency needs dictate.

9

THE CASE OF ICI

Despite the fact that large, mature organizations are notoriously difficult to change, Sir John Harvey-Jones needed only five years as chairman at Britain's Imperial Chemical Industries to alter the firm's business mix, structure, morale, and culture.[1] The resulting economic payoff was dramatic; profits in 1987 reached £1.312 billion, more than five times greater than in 1982 (see exhibit 9.1).

ICI's problems can be traced all the way back to the firm's founding in 1926 through the merger of Britain's four largest chemical companies. The company quickly became a major player in what was a worldwide cartel. Sir Harry McGowan called the ICI merger "the first step in a comprehensive scheme . . . to rationalise the chemical manufacture of the world."[2]

During the interwar years, ICI emphasized superior technology and low-cost production. Well over half of the company's university hires were scientists. The firm's position as a major player in a worldwide cartel made marketing and sales concerns almost irrelevant. The fact that the company engaged "sales

EXHIBIT 9.1

ICI'S PROFIT BEFORE TAX, 1968–1988

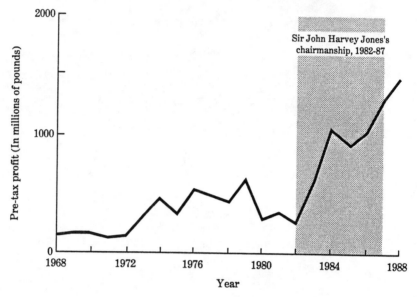

allocators" to make decisions in the "sales control department" aptly illustrated the lack of importance ICI was required to place on the market side of business.

During Britain's rearmament for World War II, ICI became tightly interlocked with the British government. To avoid being left with overcapacity after the war, ICI arranged an agreement whereby the state paid for the construction of new plants and ICI managed them for a reasonable fee. During the war, demand skyrocketed for ICI products, especially munitions, light metals, and guns.

ICI's technological victories during the years around the war were significant. Polythene, discovered in the 1930s, eventually revolutionized radar, helping Britain turn the course of the war. In the 1930s, ICI scientists helped pioneer synthetic fibers, later bringing to market Terylene, the world's first successful polyester. ICI continued to show its technical superiority in the 1950s, when the Glaswegian James Black (later Sir James Black, the winner of the 1988 Nobel Prize for Medicine) took emerging ideas about cardiovascular disease and turned them into a series of revolutionary drugs used to treat hypertension. Black's feelings about his discoveries illustrated the partiality to science that had always been an integral part of ICI's development: "The things I have been associated with happen to have made a lot of money, but commercial success has nothing to do with the quality of the science."[3]

ICI's involvement in cartels came to a halt in the years following the war, in part because of an antitrust suit brought by the United States government in reaction to the approximately eight hundred agreements ICI had signed with Du Pont to regulate competition. ICI performed poorly during the 1950s in comparison to large American and German players. The company had lost its monopoly over the chemical markets of Britain and her colonies. Further, it maintained an outmoded productive capacity and an inward-looking managerial style, both of which prevented it from taking advantage of the opportunities decartelization offered. Its economic performance in the 1960s was generally below the large U.S. competitors and average for large European competitors, and its productivity was low relative to all competitors in the 1960s and 1970s.[4]

In the 1970s, ICI's own inadequacies were compounded by unfavorable conditions throughout the United Kingdom. During the 1970s the U.K. economy suffered a lower growth rate than its Western peers, relatively high inflation, and increased labor demands (and settlements). ICI's position was affected in particular by high interest rates and the strength of the British pound between 1979 and 1982, a strength which put ICI's products at a competitive disadvantage in foreign markets. An even steeper recession between 1979 and 1984 made a company redirection simultaneously more difficult and more urgent.

One summation in 1987 of ICI's postwar performance was: "The way that ICI responded to the various challenges of the first three decades after the war reveals a great deal about its historic character. The group had immense strength, as a long list of product and process innovations testifies. But it shared some of British industry's common failings, like a poor productivity record. And it had evolved a bureaucratic style of management which avoided clear-cut responsibilities, and concentrated upon running on-going operations rather than vigorously exploiting new opportunities."[5]

*   *   *

Although each of the ICI divisions had its own cultural inheritance, there were significant commonalities across divisions and in the behavior of the corporate executive committee (traditionally called "the board"). ICI was seen as a "British institution," and was faced with the attached behavioral expectations to act in an appropriately ethical, regulated, and stable way. In the 1960s Anthony Sampson called ICI a "slumbering giant." Although moving to internationalism, the company was traditionally very British, both in sales and management. ICI's strong technical heritage made the firm somewhat unresponsive to the market in the 1970s and 1980s. The firm was full of intelligent and well-educated people who loved to debate issues, but were less enthusiastic about making needed decisions. Harvey-Jones compared the company to a huge ship plowing through the water. In his book on ICI, Andrew Pettigrew pointed out that change was customarily "evolutionary rather than revolutionary."[6]

The chairmanship between the late 1960s and Harvey-Jones's reign in the 1980s was characterized by short tenure. After Sir Paul Chambers stepped down in 1968, the next four chairmen held office for only three or four years. One senior executive pointed out the inertia induced by such turnover: "If you have a chairman who has a three-year stint in the office, the first year he's not going to lash about him too much because he wants to establish himself. The second year is a year when he can lash about, but the third year, he's already saying 'I don't want to prejudice the position of my successor,' and guys on the board are not wanting to take big risks because there's always one or two competing to be the next chairman. So if you analyze the thing you find that you only have one year in three—rather like elephants—when you can mate and make it happen."[7]

The ICI board emphasized hierarchy and status. The sixth floor of Millbank gave what one senior executive described as a feeling of "immutability, permanence, and lack of change." In financial terms, ICI typically showed a conservatism and concern for cash and capital.

The last of these organizational characteristics, fiscal conservatism, resulted in part from a cash crisis in 1966 during the reign of Sir Paul Chambers. Powerful until this crisis, Chambers began with high ideals. Similar to Harvey-Jones in that he was neither strictly a company man nor a chemist, he said in a 1964 *Sunday Times* article, "We must see . . . that our whole organisation is sensitive to growth and sensitive to change. We have changed from a narrow technical approach to a broad commercial approach." Chambers started ICI down a path of adaptation to the changing industry conditions and helped set the four broad goals that would become important in the 1960s and 1970s. The goals, destined to be abandoned because of an unfortunate economic crisis and the lingering corporate inertia, were (1) to bring ICI's technology up to the sophistication and scale of international competition of that time, (2) to improve manpower productivity of their U.K. assets, (3) to shift the geographic distribution away from the United Kingdom toward Western Europe and the Americas, and (4) to change top management organization and corporate culture to make the company more flexible and responsive to the market.[8]

Though the 1966 cash crisis was a convenient excuse to put the clamps on such redirection, a more significant inhibitor to reform was the reactive culture. In 1972, eight years after Chambers's proclamation of change, a *Sunday Times* article quoted an obviously disillusioned senior executive: "We suffer from problems of size. We employ too many highly paid people to check and cross-check other men's figures. We are an over-educated company. We still have a technical bias. We are not breeding people with an entrepreneurial flair. The Chairman has the old belief that the company can change slowly. But I think you could have a dynamic effect with proper leadership."[9]

In 1977, the Chairman's Group Conference was institutionalized, addressing among other issues the problems of short-term focus, too much managing and not enough leading, and too much focus on the United Kingdom to the detriment of ICI's international opportunities. The conference included the chairman down to the general managers. "New school" board members were beginning to have some impact, but effecting change from their small power base was still immensely difficult. Harvey-Jones said of the developments, "Out of all those board studies at this time something moved a bit but the trouble is you couldn't move the ICI system by moving a bit."[10]

Sir Maurice Hodgson, appointed chairman in 1978, embodied the intolerance of the organizational development programs and the push for cultural reforms. Shortly after assuming the chair he pronounced, "I don't want to hear about organization, all this company ever does is talk and work on organization, let's get on with business and make some money."[11]

In time, Hodgson would prove to be active in pushing for changes, if for no other reason than to respond to the upheaval in both the world economy and the chemical industry around 1980. Even more significantly, change was being driven by a rising board member with an unusual entrepreneurial flair. Pettigrew had this to say: "Harvey-Jones' arrival at Millbank as a main board director in April 1973 brought a man with a different perspective, personal style, and values into the main board; someone capable of asking questions about the role and methods of operation of the main board, the overall structure of the company, and the efficacy of the ICI and Millbank culture to meet fresh challenges of business, economic, and political change during the 1970s. The fact that Harvey-Jones was able to play this challenging role, and at the same time survive and prosper in the ICI power system, says something about his own skill as a change agent and a businessman, but also the extent of business difficulty ICI was in by the time of the 1980 recession."[12]

*   *   *

Because his father was an adviser to a maharajah, Harvey-Jones spent his first years living in luxury in India. He left for private school in England at the age of seven and enrolled in the Royal Naval College at the age of twelve. In his years immediately following his schooling, Harvey-Jones began his naval career where he eventually attained the rank of Lieutenant Commander. His Navy years contributed to the "mental and physical toughness" he claimed was so vital to becoming an effective business leader. At the age of 33, Harvey-Jones left the military so that he could spend more time with his wife and his polio-afflicted daughter. He admits that he learned all of his chemistry from a Penguin paperback. Indeed, this "outsider" perspective was one of his biggest assets over his thirty-year career at ICI.

Harvey-Jones joined ICI in 1956 as a work-study officer. After showing promise, he was quickly rewarded with the position of supply manager. Later he was moved to the business side of heavy organic chemicals (later called Petrochemicals), where he initiated a retail gasoline (petrol) business. As a deputy chairman, Harvey-Jones established invaluable credibility by reducing the substantial industrial relations problems he had inherited at the Wilton site in northeast England. The success helped to catapult him to the chairmanship of the Petrochemicals Division, where he served until 1973. His success as both deputy chairman and chairman of Petrochemicals was impressive, especially in the historical context of the Wilton site, where a lack of effective management coordination had contributed considerably to the deteriorating industrial relations situation.

Having had a significant impact (albeit temporary) on Petrochemicals, Harvey-Jones took his vision to the main board in 1973. Although he would only be publicly recognized as chairman years later, it was during this decade on the main board that Harvey-Jones laid the foundation for his eventual success. As Pettigrew notes: "I think his major role was before he became chairman. What was going on in that period from 1973 onwards was a process of softening up the old guard, and challenging some of the key values, key beliefs, and key assumptions the old guard had. . . . The real hard work had been trying to challenge and question the beliefs and tenets of the old ICI culture. You didn't do that overnight, of course. It was a very, very, long-term process, and it certainly wasn't complete in 1982 when he became chairman."[13]

Upon joining the board (the corporate executive committee), Harvey-Jones set out to drive change. He selectively utilized outside help to deliver bad news to the board, but was careful to maintain his credibility by "never missing a chance to make the point that I'm basically an operator."[14] Harvey-Jones made it easier for others to express their concerns more freely by setting up a room on the director's floor where anybody could put up a chart or make a point without having to stand up and aggressively challenge board opinion. In 1973, the newly appointed board member initiated the Petrochemicals Product Directors Advisory Committee, a group which brought together various chairmen of the Petrochemicals divisions and laid the groundwork for the heavy chemicals consolidation to follow during the next fifteen years. Through this committee and successor committees, Harvey-Jones and fellow advocate of change, board member Philip Harvey, began responding to the pressures from group chairmen. The 1977 Chairman's Group Conference signaled some progress in influencing the chairman, but while tolerance was developing at the top, leadership for change at that level was still painfully absent.

With the arrival of Hodgson to the chairmanship in 1978 came a back-to-business attitude, and some argued that Harvey-

Jones moved away from the pro-change forefront, biding his time in hopes of succeeding Hodgson. Harvey-Jones disagrees: "I certainly didn't consciously back away from the pro-change forefront and indeed, continued to advocate it during Maurice's chairmanship. I was at that time primarily involved in the merging of plastics and the petrochemicals division, which was indeed a sort of change that I saw as being necessary, coupled, I'm afraid, with a rather greater than proportionate share of the responsibility for de-manning the company at that particular time."[15]

Regardless of how active he actually was during the late 1970s, his decade of work finally paid substantial dividends in 1981 when a successor group to the 1973 Petrochemicals Products Directors Advisory Committee exerted enough pressure on the board to facilitate the merger of the Petrochemicals and Plastics divisions that he had advocated.

During the years immediately prior to Harvey-Jones's accession, a combination of forces helped set the stage for the changes the chairman-to-be eventually drove home. The petrochemicals and plastics merger was testimony to the impact Harvey-Jones and his caucus were beginning to have within the firm. In addition, a complex set of outside forces worked to prepare ICI for change. First, the Thatcher administration made it more socially acceptable to impose reform at the industrial level. Second, the increased levels of unemployment drained the power base of the trade unions, making it easier to achieve impact at the shop-floor level. Finally, the U.K. recession and the poor ICI performance made it very difficult for the ICI old guard to ignore the firm's problems.

*   *   *

Facing enormous challenge, the ICI board elected Harvey-Jones to assume the chairmanship in 1982. Although electing him for an uncharacteristic five-year term, the board displayed its conservatism by awarding themselves a renewal option after three.

Harvey-Jones's goals in the 1980s were much the same as his goals of the 1970s—he aimed to retrench the commodity business and move into a higher proportion of value-added products. To help accomplish this balance, he sought to consolidate operations in Western Europe and to make further inroads into the United States and Far East through acquisitions. Harvey-Jones hoped to push ICI into a transition from being production-driven to being market-driven. He also wanted to shift the company out of its sluggish British and ex-imperial markets and make it adaptive enough to sell wherever new customers were found.

In terms of setting this direction, Harvey-Jones later said:

The start of everything is to locate, as honestly as one can, the position of one's company and where the current trends will take one. That in itself is bound to reveal a number of outcomes consequent on pursuing present policies which are very different from those one would like. A considerable amount of scanning of the outside world, both the competitors in an individual business sense, and the external environment in a broader sense, is then necessary. Then the development of broad-scale corporate dreams must be carried out by the board. These have to be married with the individual dreams of each business who, in addition to achieving the best they can ask for their business, have to perform and deliver what the board has asked of them for the company as a whole. . . . It is far more important to be moving forward in broadly the right direction than to be stuck still without businesses going anywhere.[16]

Within a week of taking over in April of 1982, Harvey-Jones called an informal meeting of his executive team to discuss the operation of the board. This meeting produced a series of important conclusions about the board's role and mission. First, the chairman's power was increased to make him the principal executive officer, not simply the "first among equals." Second, it was agreed that the board would as a team concentrate on the strategic direction of the group, pushing decision making to those closer to the market. In the years preceding Harvey-Jones, each board member had been assigned one geographic responsibility (e.g., America), one functional responsibility (e.g., personnel), and one business area responsibility (e.g., petrochemicals). Each division consequently had one person on the board to champion its causes. This champion, along with the respective business head, formed a tight-knit policy group and devised divisional strategies. From these policy group meetings, directors wrote their recommendations and railroaded them through the board. One senior executive noted the resultant paradox: "If you won in the game, in the sense that people supported what you wanted to do, that might have been good for your business, but bad for your company. That was crazy."[17]

The policy groups fostered a parochialism that left the running of the business as a whole to the chairman and the finance director. Harvey-Jones initiated a system whereby two of the board members took care of all the divisions, three directors each took one of three major functions, and two directors handled the company's overseas affairs. Divisional chief executives began making their presentations directly to the board. Edgar Vincent, International Personnel manager, described the new system: "Executive directors no longer saw themselves as advocates on the executive team of specific businesses and their interests. The fundamental change was that the whole of the executive team was required to act as a team in listening to the proposals of a particular business, and judging the strategy and outcomes of a particular business. The team therefore became responsible for the group as a whole in a more clear and efficient way."[18]

Refocusing the board on the business as a whole gave more freedom to chief executives. Harvey-Jones, a firm believer in offering ownership to promote commitment, aimed to give divisional heads the power they craved, while increasing their accountability. Although historically ICI's country-by-country organization had its power centralized in Britain, Harvey-Jones formed nine worldwide business units, four of which were headquartered outside Britain. Though geographically dispersed, the units concerned themselves with global product lines, thus eliminating warring factions. The increased freedom and accountability made the organization more adaptive by eliminating disruptive battles over resources. Harvey-Jones noted the power in such decentralization. "Unless there is a really determined effort to 'burn the books,' and reduce this tangle of bureaucracy, the people at the bottom of the organization on whom everything depends feel an increasing lack of responsibility for the achievement of the objective. Success in the organization becomes a matter of following the rules, and it is much easier to obtain advancement and favor by avoiding mistakes than it is by actually achieving the goals so vital for business success. . . . The task of leadership is really to make the status quo more dangerous than launching into the unknown."[19]

In the first few years of his tenure, Harvey-Jones made

some other moves that clearly signaled the new era. Seeking to create better communication and recognizing the value of symbolism, Sir John quickly streamlined the board. By the end of 1982, he reduced the group from eleven members to eight. Perhaps most important, he completely eliminated the deputy chairman level in the ICI organization. Considering fluent board communications vital, Harvey-Jones questioned hierarchy: "I believe a flat organization at this level is essential, both in terms of keeping the team moving together, but also in terms of the example further down the line. After all, if a board of eight to fifteen people cannot organize themselves, except in a tiered hierarchical way, what chance have you got manning tightly down the rest of the company?"[20]

Harvey-Jones also prompted a reduction in the corporate headquarters staff from twelve hundred to four hundred, devolving many corporate responsibilities to the operating divisions. He decided ICI no longer needed the lavish headquarters at Millbank, and after toying with the idea of moving out of the building completely, offered two-thirds of the office space for sale or lease. Moreover, he set out to change the atmosphere of the board meetings. Believing the board room inhibited free exchange of ideas, Harvey-Jones moved their regular weekly meetings into what had been his office. He eliminated assigned seats, made shirt-sleeves the norm, and encouraged a general informality. At these meetings, Harvey-Jones began to insist that the ICI style of prolonged debate change. He pushed the board to be decisive and then to stop second-guessing decisions.

With Harvey-Jones's enthusiastic support, research director Charles Reece began calling together a "relevance group" early in Sir John's tenure, bringing together the resources of different divisions. In 1982, ICI realized through these groups that five different divisions were conducting colloids research. Reece initiated a colloids and surface chemicals group, one example of how the search for economies could make ICI greater than the sum of its parts.

In company restructuring, Harvey-Jones finally brought his consolidation drive to fruition in 1987, leading ICI to merge the Agriculture, Fibers, Mond, and Petrochemicals and Plastics groups into one Chemicals and Polymers Group, known as C & P. Some analysts estimated the C & P merger would save the company £50 million a year.[21] While conceding the difficulty in quantifying such savings, executives at ICI reacted favorably. One senior executive noted that expectations had "certainly been fulfilled, probably exceeded."[22] The merger also sought to prevent the slower-growth commodity businesses from dragging down the profits of the newer specialty chemicals, as well as to capitalize on the worldwide potential of the newer businesses.

In the acquisition arena, ICI effectively bought an increased international presence, particularly in specialty chemicals. The $750 million purchase of Beatrice Chemicals in 1984 gave ICI not only a significantly stronger presence in the United States, but an institutionalized acquisition team. This team helped execute the $580 million purchase of the U.S. paint company Glidden in September 1986, making ICI the top supplier of paint in the world. In 1988, ICI maintained its position as the largest supplier of surface coatings in the world, with revenues of around £1.5 billion. ICI also expanded into polyurethanes, used in insulation, car parts, and shoe soles. By 1990, these polyurethanes accounted for about $600 million a year in sales.

With such diversification, Harvey-Jones and his management team pushed ICI to a greater international balance. In 1987, the last year in which he was chairman, group sales to external customers were 25 percent in the United Kingdom (down from 39 percent in 1981), 25 percent in Continental Europe, 27 percent in the Americas, 17 percent in Australia, Japan, and the Far East, and 6 percent elsewhere. This balance left ICI less vulnerable to domestic economic downturns.

In many ways, Harvey-Jones made this huge transformation look easy. It was not. Some old-time board members dragged their feet whenever possible. As fast as Harvey-Jones could excite people in middle and lower management, their bosses were sometimes just as swift in killing that new energy. Because ICI's quest for higher productivity reduced its U.K. work force from 74,700 in 1981 to 56,230 in 1987, a 25 percent drop, labor unions were especially critical. Roger Lyons, spokesman for the Association of Scientific, Technical, & Managerial Staffs summarized the discontent. "They publish these interviews as if he's Father Christmas. I can tell you, in Manchester, he's not. . . . We see him as the human face at the head of the dole queue."[23] But because of the way that Harvey-Jones and his team handled layoffs, "There was, literally, virtually no industrial relations upset or major problems connected with those programs—it was a huge achievement, an amazing achievement."[24] Harvey-Jones ardently supported ICI's well-established policy of achieving manpower reductions through early retirement, outplacement, and retraining programs backed by generous severance payments.

Harvey-Jones's impact on morale at ICI is generally seen as tremendous. Not only did the employees who remained with the company generally feel that their former workmates lost in reductions were treated fairly, but they were comforted with the security of working for a firm that seemed to be rock solid and poised for the future. For this, they greatly respected their chairman. Between his television appearances and business visits, Harvey-Jones also put a personal touch to a company known for its immutability. As one company veteran noted: "He was able to have a very clear focus for people to identify with. It's very important that people identify with the objectives and purpose that are being enunciated by the chairman. The identification with Harvey-Jones was almost at the personal level. [Employees] didn't think of him as chairman so much as they thought of him as the leader—and a guy they could respect—because he was able to relate to all the people."[25] Harvey-Jones was well known for treating all levels with respect. In 1986, for example, he visited ICI pharmaceuticals in Macclesfield to meet with the shop steward and union members in response to their personal invitation.

Approaching his retirement from ICI, Harvey-Jones commented on how he felt he should be evaluated. "My success or failure will be, not in where the company will be [when I leave], but where it will be in five years' time. The work I have been doing has not been to get a quick bang out of the market, but to change the direction of the company."[26] Altering the direction of the firm required cultural change, and best evidence as of 1990 suggests that some change clearly did occur, although it is too early to judge how deeply. Although the rapid increases in ICI's profitability cannot all be attributed to the new culture, performance since his departure suggests that the culture (not just Harvey-Jones's leadership) must have played some part; profit before taxes in 1989 climbed even higher to a record £1,470 million.

*   *   *

The ICI story is interesting for our purposes because it is in many ways prototypical of the ten instances of cultural change that we studied. Here, as with virtually all the other cases, increasing competition in a difficult business environment (at ICI, due to oil shocks and a tough U.K. economy) created larger and larger misfits between a firm's corporate culture and its context (see exhibit 9.2). As they grew, these nonalignments acted as a significant drag on the firm's economic performance. Yet despite the bad results, historical events had left the culture so unadaptive that it resisted most needed changes until the arrival of John Harvey-Jones as chairman (see exhibit 9.3).

Chosen both because of his credibility and because he had been making the case for change, Harvey-Jones used his capac-

EXHIBIT 9.2

THE EVOLUTION OF A STRATEGICALLY INAPPROPRIATE
CULTURE AT ICI

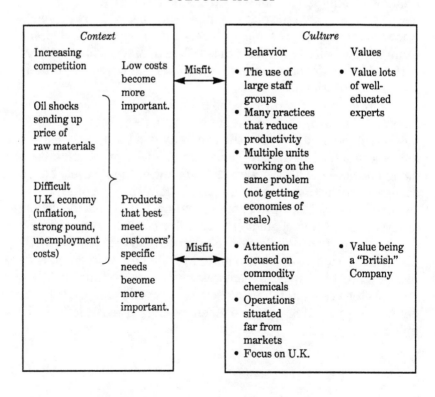

ity for leadership to help initiate hundreds of actions that, collectively, began to move the culture. He also drew attention to himself as a highly identifiable figure that stood for a new order at ICI (see exhibit 9.4) and inspired hundreds (perhaps thousands) of managers to initiate still more change-producing actions.

How much ICI's corporate culture was altered during Jones's tenure is hard to determine at this writing. It seems clear, however, that the net result of all this activity was powerful enough to make the corporate culture somewhat more adaptive.

EXHIBIT 9.3

THE EVOLUTION OF AN UNADAPTIVE CULTURE AT ICI

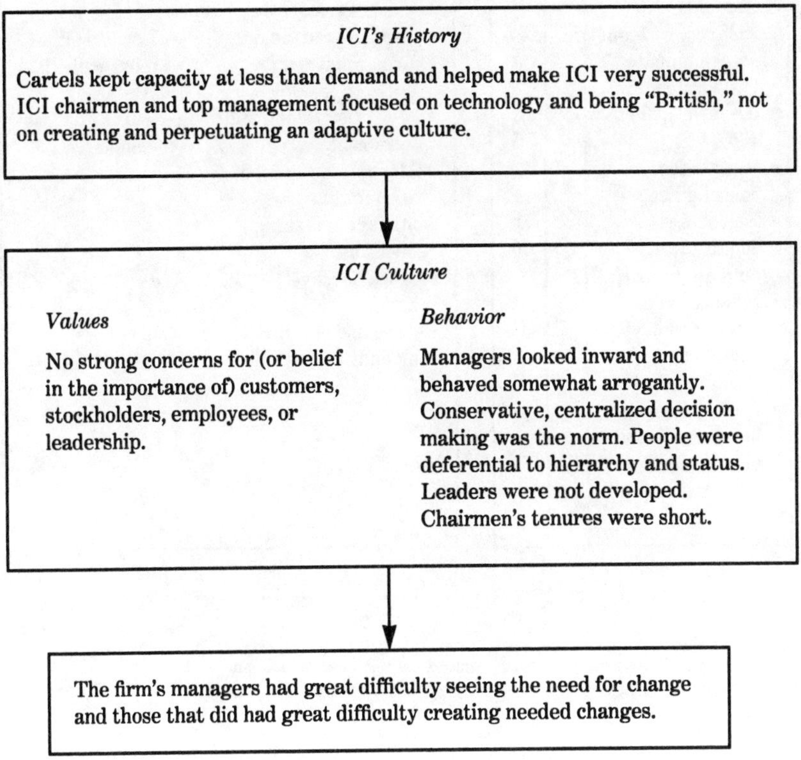

ICI's History

Cartels kept capacity at less than demand and helped make ICI very successful. ICI chairmen and top management focused on technology and being "British," not on creating and perpetuating an adaptive culture.

ICI Culture

Values

No strong concerns for (or belief in the importance of) customers, stockholders, employees, or leadership.

Behavior

Managers looked inward and behaved somewhat arrogantly. Conservative, centralized decision making was the norm. People were deferential to hierarchy and status. Leaders were not developed. Chairmen's tenures were short.

The firm's managers had great difficulty seeing the need for change and those that did had great difficulty creating needed changes.

EXHIBIT 9.4

CULTURAL CHANGE AT ICI, 1982–1987

Actions

- Top team reorganized, pushing decision making down
- Board meetings moved out of board room
- Divisions reorganized into nine worldwide businesses—four headquartered outside U.K.
- Size of board reduced, with one level eliminated
- Corporate staff cut from 1,200 to 400
- Businesses consolidated
- Businesses acquired outside the U.K.
- New vision and strategies for ICI communicated continuously
- Harvey-Jones becomes a very visible model of new strategy and culture

ICI's PERFORMANCE IMPROVES

Changes in ICI's Corporate Culture

Behavior

- More high productivity practices
- Less waste due to duplication of effort
- More international focus
- More attention to customers' needs
- More customer visits
- More focus on high value added products
- More attention to market trends
- Less inward looking
- Less conservative decision making
- More risk taking and leadership
- More decentralized with middle managers making decisions
- More decisive actions
- Less use of formal/ elegant offices

Values*

- More value placed on profits/ stockholders
- More value placed on customers
- Leadership more valued. Hierarchy and status less valued

* Not clear yet how widely these are shared within senior management.

10

THE CASE OF NISSAN

When the word culture is used in reference to Japanese firms, it almost inevitably has a positive connotation.[1] Because of the success of Japan over the past few decades and the mystique surrounding that success, one might conclude that major Japanese firms never develop problem cultures. But this is not true. The case of Nissan is a good example.[2]

Nissan's roots go back to 1911 when Masujiro Hashimoto, an American-trained engineer, founded the Kaishinsha Motor Car Works in Tokyo. Lacking capital, he gained the financial support of three men whose last names began with the letters, D, A, and T. He honored them by naming his first car the *DAT*, which literally means "escaping rabbit" in Japanese. In 1918, he produced the son of DAT, or the Datson, which was renamed the *Datsun* because the word "son" in Japanese means damage or loss. In the 1920s, Hashimoto's company merged with several other firms and eventually, in 1933, became Nissan.

By most measures, Nissan did exceptionally well in its early years. On the eve of World War II, it had grown to be the second largest automaker in Japan. After the war, it struggled initially, but then grew rapidly again (see exhibit 10.1). At first, almost all the growth was in Japan, although the firm did embark on a joint venture in the United Kingdom in 1955 and had experienced some success with its small trucks in the United States in the early 1960s. But by the late 1960s, Nissan was exporting over 300,000 vehicles or 26 percent of its total production.

As the firm's extraordinary growth continued in the 1970s, it began to suffer from what future Nissan President Yutaka Kume has called the "big corporation disease." With growth came additional layers in the chain of command, which prevented issues from coming to the attention of top management quickly and efficiently. This reduced the efficiency and accuracy of decision making at the board level. Growth also greatly increased specialization and departmentalization, which encouraged sectionalism and parochial decision making. To keep the increasingly large organization under control, the personnel department came up with elaborate rules and regulations, which

EXHIBIT 10.1

NISSAN SALES
(IN THOUSANDS OF YEN)

Years	Revenues
1935	4,359
1940	80,532
1945	42,826
1950	13,364,828
1955	14,247,257
1960	54,800,916
1965	213,418,000
1970	669,000,000
1975	1,429,600,000

buried employees in an organizational structure that often drained their willingness and readiness to work hard.

These problems were compounded by labor difficulties. The company took a hard line against its strong leftist union in 1953, employing lockout techniques and other measures. Workers responded with a hundred-day general strike. Katsuji Kawamata, who later became president of Nissan in 1957, was assigned to deal with the problem. He relied upon Ichiro Shioji, a union leader, to settle the dispute. Kawamata's debt to Shioji grew after the labor leader took care of Prince's union when Nissan merged with that automaker in 1965. After Takashi Ishihara became president in 1977, he tried to regain managerial control from Shioji, which raised tensions between management and the union. However, Shioji successfully retained power at Nissan until 1986 when he retired as the leader of the labor union. Many Nissan managers felt that Shioji's influence was destructive and that a number of the firm's problems in the 1970s and 1980s stemmed from these disputes and the bad relationship between management and labor. Trying to resolve these problems encouraged Nissan's management to focus inwardly instead of looking outward to the changing market and customer needs.

These problems of size and labor relations began to show up after 1972 in declining market share statistics and four years later in a flattening of net income (see exhibits 10.2 and 10.3). Domestic market share slid from 33.7 percent in 1972 to 25.6 percent in 1985. Meanwhile, Toyota's market share increased from 39.6 percent in 1976 to 42 percent in 1985. The gap in share between the two companies rose ominously, from 5.9 percent in 1976 to 16.4 percent in 1985.[3]

For the most part, Nissan's difficulties grew incrementally and slowly, like the gap in domestic market share. One visible exception was the failure of the Stanza in 1981. This was Nissan's first strategic front-wheel drive car. Its disappointing showing in the marketplace led to more conservative styling and design decisions, which, in turn, attracted few young customers. The lack of a successful car aimed at young drivers in conjunction with rumors about the problems at Nissan led to a slide in the firm's ranking as a desirable employer among college students from fifteenth to fortieth place.

During this period Nissan watchers became increasingly critical of the firm's corporate culture, which was often described

EXHIBIT 10.2

NISSAN MOTOR COMPANY'S PERCENTAGE OF DOMESTIC
MARKET SHARE

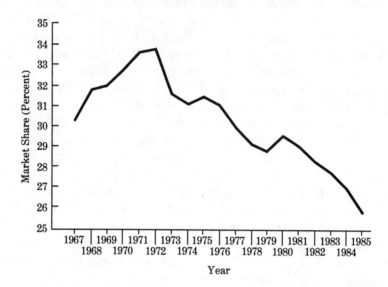

as too inward-looking, bureaucratic, and autocratic.[4] Some won-
dered whether such a culture could be changed, and whether
Nissan would therefore continue to wither in an increasingly
competitive worldwide auto industry. Others believed that
change was possible with the right leadership at the top. And in
mid-1985, they saw evidence that such leadership was taking
command.

*   *   *

In June of 1985, Yutaka Kume assumed the presidency of Nissan, replacing Ishihara who then became chairman. Kume was
born in 1921 and graduated in 1944 from the University of Tokyo
with a B.E. in aircraft engineering. He joined Nissan in 1946
and began working in the production control and engineering
area. In 1964 he became general manager of that area at the
Zama Plant, and in 1971 was made general manager of the Yoshi-
wara Plant. In 1973 he was promoted to director and member of
the board and concurrently served as general manager of the
Tochigi Plant. In 1977 Kume became managing director in
charge of the office of product and engineering strategy and
remained as general manager at the Tochigi Plant until the end

EXHIBIT 10.3

NISSAN'S NET INCOME, 1970–1985
(IN THOUSANDS OF DOLLARS)

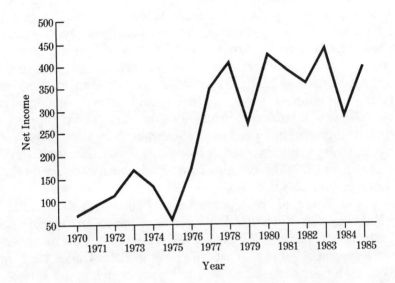

of 1978. In 1979 he took charge of the office of product and engineering strategy. Through the late 1960s and 1970s, Kume was an instrumental figure in the modernization of the company's manufacturing facilities, including the rationalization of production and the improvement of productivity. In 1983, Kume became the executive vice president in charge of research and development, diversified operations, and the corporate planning office, and concurrently served as the general manager of the quality assurance division. In 1984, with his backing, some of the management at the Nissan Technical Center (NTC) started to develop a new design process that would foster greater creativity.[5]

Both Kume's education and his career path contrast sharply with his two predecessors. Ishihara (president from 1977 to 1985) was trained in law and spent his early career years at Nissan working in accounting, finance, and sales. Kawamata (president from 1957 to 1973) worked for the Industrial Bank of Japan for nearly twenty years before coming to Nissan.

In August 1985, two months after Kume was named president, thirteen middle-level managers from Nissan Technical

Center's development department, in collaboration with an out-side consulting firm, McKinsey & Company, formed a task force called the Product Market Strategy Group (PMSG). Zenzo Son-oda, the head of R&D and a friend of Kume, supported their concept of changing the atmosphere at the Technical Center and influenced top management to agree to such an investigation. Concerned that the culture at the NTC was stifling and bureau-cratic, and that workers spent most of their time trying to co-ordinate activities and pushing paper rather than focusing on trying to produce a good car, these middle-level managers set out to create a better environment—one that would support a certain degree of independence, encourage delegation of author-ity and responsibility, and remove any hesitation lower-level management might have about questioning rules or promoting open communications.

As a result of the discoveries and the suggestions of the PMSG task force, the R&D department began introducing or-ganizational change in January 1986. Until then, R&D managers were responsible for at least three car models. Under the new system, a manager looked after only one model, which allowed him to follow the car through all stages of development—from design to planning for production, marketing, and sales—and to focus his attention on building a car that would satisfy customers for the least possible expense. To further encourage a customer orientation, R&D general managers were put into three market-oriented groups. To reduce design time and increase quality, simultaneous engineering was introduced—where each depart-ment was asked to pass on information at the earliest possible stage of development to all other departments.

With the encouragement of the PMSG task force, managers at NTC developed a number of additional ideas which were then implemented over the next few years. One scheme called for a yearly event in which the center would open its doors to the public to show off the design studio, show crash tests, and give driving demonstrations. Another called for an essay competition and a new business concept contest, both designed to reward and promote innovative ideas. To reduce the status difference between bosses and subordinates, NTC management agreed to abolish the serial numbers (indicating rank) displayed on the name badges worn by all Nissan employees. NTC managers also decided to make uniforms optional, believing that freedom of dress and expression would add to creativity and innovation in their work as stylists and designers. To further promote an atmosphere of increased creativity, they introduced the idea of "flex time," where people were required to be at work only from 10:30 to 3:30 P.M. and could arrive early or leave late as they preferred.

To help employees pay more attention to the competition, NTC management introduced a policy allowing design employees to own a competitor's car. In the past, Nissan employees could not own competitors' cars. In fact, Nissan did not allow any outsiders to come onto company grounds if they were driving a non-Nissan car. To help employees become more interested in the "big picture" of car making, management at NTC set up a program called the Challenge Creation Club to fund certain kinds of activities (e.g., the Italian Car Club) that would provide employees with "extracurricular" ways to meet other people and exchange ideas.

At the same time that these concepts were being developed at NTC, Kume began to bring his senior management together in "top forum" meetings to discuss the larger issues facing the company. About eighty people participated in these biannual sessions, each of which lasted three days and two nights. The earliest of these meetings occurred while Nissan was reporting a loss for the first half of FY 1986–87 of 19.7 billion yen. The last previously reported loss was in 1951.

Against this background, in December of 1986, Kume issued a statement of "corporate philosophy." In an unusual and obviously important communiqué to all Nissan employees, he emphasized four principles: "We must keep in touch with the global market, creating attractive products through our innovative and reliable technology. . . . We must be sensitive to customers' needs and offer them maximum satisfaction based on steadfast sincerity and ceaseless efforts to meet their requirements. . . . We must focus on global trends, making the world the stage for our activities, and to nurture a strong company that will grow with the times. . . . We must foster the development of an active and vital group of people who are ready and willing at all times to take on the challenge of achieving new goals."

To help make this philosophy a reality throughout Nissan, a new coordinating group called the Product Market Strategy

Division was established at company headquarters in January 1987. The main purpose of the PMSD was to facilitate the integration of the disparate functions and divisions involved in designing, producing, testing, and marketing a car. In the past, planning had been split between sales and design; sales planning had been a part of the domestic sales department, and design planning had been a part of R&D. These groups had different agendas, leading to conflicting design and marketing plans. According to Takashi Hisatomi, the general manager of the Product Market Strategy Office, "[We were] established in the middle of the sales department and the R&D department. We now manage the power struggle between the two. . . . We have to decide everything from the viewpoint of the customer. That is the point of our department."[6]

The hundred members of this Product Market Strategy Division were split into four sections. The first, the Product Market Strategy Office, coordinated the activity within the department and initiated long-term planning and strategy. Workers in this office researched general markets and tried to spot developing trends. When they discovered a trend, they would develop a concept to fit the market need and conceive long- and middle-term planning for that concept. The three other sections specialized in short-term planning and the logistics of car development. They were divided according to product/market type. The Z10 group handled the family cars or sedans such as the Bluebird (Stanza) and the Cedric. The Z20 group developed small cars like the Micra and the Pulsar. The third group, Z30, focused on specialty cars or sporty models like the Silvia (240sx) and the 300zx. The product manager system created in 1986 at Nissan's technical center was used in all three groups; one manager followed a car from R&D through manufacturing and sales.

The combination of this reorganization and Kume's philosophy statement sent a powerful signal throughout Nissan that change was needed and expected. Kume personally began carrying this message in visits and speeches to employees with a volume of communication that was unprecedented for a Nissan president.

*   *   *

Starting in 1987, shortly after the establishment of the Product

Market Strategy Division, Nissan headquarters began to delegate more authority to the plants. Over a period of five years, the amount of money that plant heads could control without the involvement of headquarters increased tenfold. In return, each plant was asked to devise its own system of promoting performance and the "customer first" philosophy.

At the Zama facility, managers created a sophisticated management information system that measured quality, delivery, and cost factors on a common matrix at the section level (a typical section might have three hundred employees). This accounting system allowed more delegation because it gave section managers a meaningful bottom line that they could control—a bottom line that took into account variables relevant to both profitability and customer satisfaction. With the help of this system, costs at Zama decreased by 20 percent from 1985 to 1988, while quality increased by 70 percent and delivery time decreased by 70 percent.

At the Zama Plant, managers also attempted to bring Nissan closer to the customer in direct ways. They hosted events called Open Days when people who were not associated with Nissan were free to walk around the plant grounds. According to Haruyoshi Takagishi, deputy general manager, production control and engineering department, "We have usually used the space in front of the building. We ask the local people to open up shops and sell food and clothing for the day. It is like a bazaar." The plant also sponsored small sporting events, such as soccer matches and baseball games, and invited the teams to use the facilities within the Zama Plant grounds. Through endeavors like these, management felt they were better received in Zama city and that this even paid off in increased car sales. Nissan's market share in 1985 was 25 percent in Zama city, while Toyota's was 40 percent. In 1990, Nissan's share increased to 40 percent while Toyota's had dropped to 25 percent.

Corporate personnel initiated two significant changes in their efforts to implement Kume's new philosophy. First, they increased the amount of interdepartmental rotation of employees (Kume felt that the shuffling of managers created more action-oriented people). Second, they changed promotion and pay policies traditionally based on seniority to ones based more on performance (Kume felt that evaluating performance rather than seniority would place the proper emphasis on action and merit).

Nissan's sales organization was not as aggressive in trying to create the new culture as some other parts of the firm, but sales management eventually made two important changes. They established a customer complaint desk in every dealership in Japan. They also began financing the construction of new showrooms for their dealers to create a more attractive, inviting environment.[7]

By 1990, as these efforts gained momentum, departments throughout Nissan began to change how they operated, even those at lower levels in the organization. The case of the Nissan Vehicle Experiment department may be typical. This group test drives new cars. According to department head Kenzo Hirashima:

> We are now intensifying our efforts to learn why what we thought was good has received complaints from customers. For instance, in the U.S. there is a certain road surface which does not exist in Japan. Because of the way the highway is built, it has a sequence of small bumps over a long distance. We had simulated such a road surface here at our test grounds, but only for a shorter sequence of bumps. We thought our U.S. cars were satisfactory based on our simulation. However, when driving on that road surface in the U.S., we learned that it becomes unbearably uncomfortable for the driver, which is why we received complaints. Therefore, we have decided that we should actually drive on that surface in the U.S. to test the comfort of those cars.

The idea of making sure that the tests they performed had meaning in the real world of the customer represented a basic transformation in the way this department approached its dealings with the market.

*   *   *

The first product to benefit from the changes at Nissan was the Silvia (called the 240sx in the United States). Launched in May 1988, this sporty compact coupe with comfortable seating for four was targeted at twenty-five-year-olds and sold for a little less than two million yen (or $12,000). Winning the 1988/89 Japan Car of the Year award and the Good Design grand prize awarded by the Ministry of International Trade and Industry (MITI), the Silvia combined innovative styling and technology, captivating the nation's youth.

Silvia's previous model had been unsuccessful, selling only about two hundred units per month in 1987. Because many believed that sales could not be any worse, managers felt more comfortable taking a chance and letting young designers have free rein over the new model. Challenged by the failure of the 1985 Skyline and the fiscal losses of 1986, a consensus developed to let only young employees work on the Silvia because the car was targeted toward a young market. The average age of the people who eventually became involved in the project was twenty-eight.

Discovering that pure market research dictated that they develop a car that would have been an exact replica of the Honda Prelude, the dominating vehicle in its class at the time, designers instead tried to think about what the category and the car provided to the customer. They concentrated more on emotions and feelings in attempting to create the perfect car. Because the young staff could provide a better understanding of the young customer, they became vital to the project. Koichiro Kawamura, the manager in charge of the Silvia stated: "I frequently told our young designers and sales department staff to create a car that they would want to buy."

Kawamura tried to generate an atmosphere of creativity and individual expression amongst those who worked on the Silvia. Allowing the young designers to discuss the product and make decisions about it without the interference of top management was an important step in this process. According to Kenji Shimokaze, a manager in the business research department, "The Silvia was the first example where young managers really made decisions and also where we invited an outside fashion designer to help with the model."

The new Product Market Strategy Division coordinated all aspects of Silvia's development from inception to sales. One manager, Koichiro Kawamura, oversaw the entire development of the product, thus ensuring the consistency of the designer's vision throughout the process. This form of decentralized decision making represented a break from tradition in Nissan's centralized bureaucracy. According to Satoshi Matsutomi, who worked as a designer on the Silvia, "Mr. Kawamura, the manager at that time for the Silvia, had the final decision concerning all aspects of Silvia's design. Since he was older, he would ask young staff members including me for advice. Usually, he implemented the results of such young people's opinions." Top executives with no official role in the model were not allowed to influence the design of the product. Mr. Matsutomi remarked on the previous practice: "I have experienced a few occasions in the design room when we had to change the headlights of a car because some executive came and said: 'I don't like that one, change it.' These last-minute changes no longer occur. With the old culture, subordinates were always looking at those above them in the hierarchy. No matter the content of the issue, they would just say 'yes' to whatever they were told to do." This change was reinforced by Kume himself who backed away from choosing the final model of the Silvia.[8] According to Matsutomi, "Mr. Kume came, looked at the two clay models, and just walked away. We literally had to run to catch up to him. We told him which one of the models we preferred and asked if that was all right. He just nodded. On previous occasions he would probably have told us which model would go into production. But this time he didn't say anything."

The Silvia was produced at the Kyushu Plant, which had been desperate for work. Since Nissan as a rule did not fire or lay off workers when times were tough, over a thousand employees at the Kyushu Plant (at least a quarter of the work force) had been transferred to other plants, many leaving families behind. Other workers were occupied with tasks such as cleaning the plant grounds and the factory. When the chance came to produce a new and potentially important car, the workers were generally very enthusiastic. They were further encouraged by visits from Kume and senior managing directors. Since Kyushu was far from Tokyo, such visits were very unusual.

The Silvia was not only designed by youthful employees, it was also sold by them. One employee commented, "What was unique with the Silvia was that when discussing sales promotion in the meetings, we did not have to have the presence of older managers. All of us younger employees could get together and discuss freely what we thought about the car. All we had to do was to report the results to our manager. So we were free to say whatever we thought. These discussion sessions led to new ideas." In addition, young people worked on direct sales of the Silvia in the dealerships. According to Masaharu Tomosada, deputy general manager of the Product Market Strategy Office, "Unlike the conventional way, we requested that each of these dealers come up with a 'Silvia

Leader' who would be the main person responsible for Silvia
sales toward the end users. We also asked that those 'leaders'
be in their twenties." Concentrating responsibility on these
young people to sell a car aimed at a young market represented a new approach to sales.

After the announcement and launch of the new Silvia model,
ten "caravan" teams of two people, a young man and a young
woman, left the Kyushu Plant in new Silvia cars, taking ten days
to reach Tokyo. Along the way they promoted the car and visited thirty dealers, encouraging them, expressing pride in the
vehicle, and trying to make a personal appeal to the dealers to
sell the car. They received a very positive response. Toshiya
Yamamoto recalled:

> On our way [to Tokyo], many people would approach the
> campaign car and say 'what a wonderful car, please give us
> a catalogue on this car.' The young couple would hand out
> business cards and catalogues to whomever seemed inter-
> ested. Those people who drove the Silvia campaign cars
> cannot forget the sensation of being received as stars. Even
> now they still get together and hold Silvia group par-
> ties. . . . [D]uring this caravan, one of the cars developed a
> transmission problem at the Yokohama Chinatown. The
> Shizuoka prefecture plant supplied the new transmission,
> but the technology was only available at the technical cen-
> ter at Atsugi. The sales department was in Tokyo at the
> headquarters, and assembly was conducted at the Yoko-
> hama Plant. People from these four different locations all
> got together and repaired the car overnight so that the car
> was ready to go at about 6:00 the next morning. When it
> started, everyone applauded. . . . On the tenth day, we
> arranged that these cars would arrive in front of the Nissan
> Headquarters building around lunchtime so all the employ-
> ees could gather and greet the cars. We were planning to
> have Mr. Saito, who was the executive in charge of this
> caravan project, make a speech. But somebody suggested
> that we should have Mr. Kume make the greeting. In the
> morning we went up to his office and asked him. He ac-
> cepted such a proposal and appeared in the uniform for the
> caravan project to make the speech.

After a successful launch, the young people marketing the Silvia decided to increase customer follow-up. When the Silvia received the Car-of-the-Year award, they sent a letter of gratitude to those who had originally purchased the car. They felt that word-of-mouth promotion was an important aspect of Silvia's marketing.

When the new model was introduced, President Kume publicly announced that it would beat its direct competitor, the Honda Prelude. In fact, it immediately captured 3.3 percent of the domestic (Japanese) market, selling 26,279 cars in the first half of the year, while the Prelude sold 30,353 cars. In the second half of 1988, Silvia's market share rose to 3.8 percent (34,705 cars) while the Honda Prelude dropped to 1.1 percent (10,282 cars). By the second half of 1989, sales of the Silvia were 44,143 compared to the 16,979 Preludes sold by Honda.

*   *   *

In many ways, the situations at Nissan and ICI in the early 1980s were very different, reflecting differences in the home countries, the two industries, the histories of the firms, and the specific personalities involved. Yet there are important similarities here, themes that we also see in the other cases of cultural change. Both firms achieved great success in the middle of the century. With growth, both developed cultures that were not very adaptive. As competition increased and the conditions in their industries became tougher in the later 1970s and early 1980s, both experienced performance problems. In the 1980s, both got unconventional (for them) top managers that led the charge for change.

In Nissan's case, Kume empowered like-minded managers at Nissan Technical Center, an organization that reported to him before he was appointed president. He then worked on his own top eighty executives. When he felt the time was right, he announced the new corporate philosophy, allowed the restructuring at the corporate level, helped select the Silvia as a likely project where new strategies could flourish and produce successful results, and then encouraged changes in manufacturing, personnel, sales, and elsewhere. As a result of those actions, hundreds of changes were initiated that, collectively, began to improve the firm's performance and then to shift the culture away from its inward-looking, autocratic, and bureaucratic tendencies (see exhibit 10.4).

EXHIBIT 10.4

CULTURAL CHANGE AT NISSAN

Examples of Specific Actions Taken by Nissan Managers

- New structure at NTC (three market oriented groups).
- Open events for public at NTC, Zama, and elsewhere.
- Managers at NTC allowed to own competitors cars.
- PMSD organized in three market groups.
- Zama supports sports teams for surrounding communities.
- New complaint desk in every Japanese dealership.
- Sales helps finance construction of new showrooms in dealerships.
- Nissan Vehicle Experiment Dept. test drives U.S. cars in the United States on actual road surfaces.
- Outside design help used for Silvia.

- New structure at NTC (one new car per manager).
- Simultaneous engineering at NTC.
- Essay competition and new business development contest at NTC.
- Rank no longer indicated on name badges at NTC.
- Flex time available at NTC.
- Challenge creation clubs at NTC.
- PMSD puts one person lower in hierarchy in charge of each new car.
- Plants given discretion for budgets ten times as large as in past.
- New accounting system at Zama allows more delegation.
- Corporate personnel increases rotation of managers.
- Corporate personnel make performance evaluations less focused on seniority and more on performance.
- Young teams assigned to Silvia.
- Senior management not allowed to interfere with Silvia.

Improved Performance

- Quality, cost, and delivery time change at Zama.
- Success of Silvia.
- Many awards for lineup of new cars

- Slide in domestic market share stopped.
- Net income up.

Cultural Change

- Less inward looking.
- More customer focused.

- Less autocratic and bureaucratic.
- More initiative, leadership, and creativity from below.

How much has Nissan changed? In 1990, managers at the firm gave varying estimates. Some believed Nissan had come about 30 percent of the way toward the culture they needed. Others thought the company had come as far as 60 percent of the way. However, no one felt that the job was completed. According to President Kume, "Six years have passed and I believe we are now about halfway through this process of changing the corporate culture. I think it might take more than six more years to finish the job. Working out the problems of the first stage is easier; after that it becomes more difficult. In the process of change, we have reached a plateau. During this early stage, people think that Nissan has changed a great deal, but we shouldn't take what they say at face value."

Takashi Hisatomi, general manager of the Product Market Strategy Office, concurred with Kume's assessment. He also noted that the sense of crisis which had motivated a great deal of the change had passed. He commented: "Five years ago we used the fact that we were on the verge of crisis to gain energy to change. This time we can't use such a strategy. Previously it was a fight for survival, now we are fighting a more offensive, aggressive battle."

In terms of measurable results, the picture was generally characterized by positives. In 1990, Nissan dominated *Road and Track*'s list of the ten best cars in the world and its list of the ten best car values, with seven of the twenty overall spots. In the previous decade, Nissan had failed to appear even once on these polls. Nissan also captured two of the top ten spots in the individual model category of J.D. Power & Associates' Initial Quality Survey of new cars. After falling almost steadily for fifteen years, Nissan's domestic market share also rose in 1988 and 1989 (but not by much, from 23.6 percent to 23.7 percent). U.S. market share also increased—from 4.8 percent in 1988 to 5.2 percent in 1989. More dramatically, between 1987 and 1990, net income rose from ¥20 billion to ¥116 billion ($165 million to $940 million).[9]

IV

Summary and Conclusions

11

ON THE ROLE OF TOP MANAGEMENT

Culture represents an interdependent set of values and ways of behaving that are common in a community and that tend to perpetuate themselves, sometimes over long periods of time. This continuity is the product of a variety of social forces that are frequently subtle, bordering on invisible, through which people learn a group's norms and values, are rewarded when they accept them, and are ostracized when they do not. The importance of this phenomenon has been recognized for decades. The research reported in this book demonstrates the specific power of culture in one setting: inside companies. Our studies clearly show that certain kinds of corporate cultures help, while others undermine, long-term economic performance.

Although it is widely believed today that strong cultures create excellent performance, we have found that the recent experiences of nearly two hundred firms do not support that theory. In firms with strong corporate cultures, managers tend to march energetically in the same direction in a well-coordinated fashion. That alignment, motivation, organization, and control can help performance, but only if the resulting actions fit an intelligent business strategy for the specific environment in which a firm operates. Performance will not be enhanced if the common behaviors and methods of doing business do not fit the needs of a firm's product or service market, financial market, and labor market. Strong cultures with practices that do not fit a company's context can actually lead intelligent people to behave in ways that are destructive—that systematically undermine an organization's ability to survive and prosper.

Furthermore, our research shows that even contextually or strategically appropriate cultures will not promote excellent performance over long periods unless they contain norms and values that can help firms adapt to a changing environment. We have found a number of prominent companies that performed adequately from strong market positions in slowly changing environments during the 1940s, 1950s, and 1960s, but that have not done well in the past ten to twenty years when the business world became more competitive and faster moving. In each of these cases, we have also found change-resistant cultures.

Cultures that are not adaptive take many forms. In large corporations, they are often characterized by some arrogance, insularity, and bureaucratic centralization, all supported by a value system that cares more about self-interest than about customers, stockholders, employees, or good leadership. In such cultures, managers tend to ignore relevant contextual changes and to cling to outmoded strategies and ossified practices. They make it difficult for anyone else, especially those below them in the hierarchy, to implement new and better strategies and practices. And they tend to turn people off—particularly those individuals whose personal values include an emphasis on integrity, trust, and caring for other human beings.

In corporate cultures that promote useful change, managers pay close attention to relevant changes in a firm's context and then initiate incremental changes in strategies and practices to keep firms and cultures in line with environmental realities. These behavioral norms seem to be driven by a value system that stresses meeting the legitimate needs of all the key constituencies whose cooperation is essential to business performance—especially customers, employees, and stockholders. These values also emphasize the importance of people and processes that can create change—especially competent leadership throughout the management hierarchy. Such a value system, when expressed in written form, often sounds either hopelessly idealistic, or vague to the point of uselessness, or even inappropriately religious (e.g., "Treat others as you would have them treat you"). Yet that very value system is the key to excellent performance nowadays because it tends to energize managers and get them to do what is needed to help firms adapt to a changing competitive environment (see exhibit 11.1).

Many companies today say that they care about customers, stockholders, and employees. More and more organizations nowadays say they believe in the importance of competent leadership at multiple levels in their hierarchies. But few really do, at least in a cultural sense—where who gets promoted says more

EXHIBIT 11.1

ADAPTIVE VS. UNADAPTIVE CORPORATE CULTURES*

	Adaptive Corporate Cultures	Unadaptive Corporate Cultures
Core Values	Most managers care deeply about customers, stockholders, and employees. They also strongly value people and processes that can create useful change (e.g., leadership up and down the management hierarchy)	Most managers care mainly about themselves, their immediate work group, or some product (or technology) associated with that work group. They value the orderly and risk-reducing management process much more highly than leadership initiatives
Common Behavior	Managers pay close attention to all their constituencies, especially customers, and initiate change when needed to serve their legitimate interests, even if that entails taking some risks	Managers tend to behave somewhat insularly, politically, and bureaucratically. As a result, they do not change their strategies quickly to adjust to or take advantage of changes in their business environments

* This is repeat of exhibit 4.3.

about real values than any mission statement or credo. On average, those few that do seem to be outperforming most others by a considerable margin.

*   *   *

When performance-enhancing cultures emerge in start-up situations, at least two elements seem to be critical: (1) an entrepreneur who has (or develops) a business philosophy that is similar to what we have found at the core of adaptive cultures and (2) a business strategy that fits the specific situation and that produces sufficient success to make the entrepreneur (and his or her philosophy) highly credible to the employees. We suspect these elements are not unusual in highly successful young companies, mostly because they are necessary for success in a competitive business environment. But we also have evidence that performance-enhancing cultures often erode over time, either because they are not effectively passed on to the hoards of new managers needed in a growing business or because time and success and other factors blur people's memories about why they were successful in the first place (see exhibit 11.2).

We have considerable data on the creation of performance-enhancing cultures in mature organizations that lacked such cultures. In general, this seems to happen infrequently and with great difficulty. In mature firms, even modestly unadaptive cultures can resist change with great intensity. Overcoming this tendency requires a specific combination of personal attributes and actions—a combination that appears to be all too rare today.

In the cases of successful change that we have studied, we have always found one or two unusually capable leaders on top. These individuals had track records for producing dramatic results. They also combined the "outsider's" objective view of their firms with the credibility and power base usually associated with insiders.

These leaders began the process of creating change soon after their appointment as president, chairman, or division general manager. They did so first by establishing a sense of crisis or need for change, and then by creating a new direction for their firms based on a constituencies-are-king philosophy and contextually appropriate business strategies. They challenged the status quo with very basic questions: Is this what customers really need and want? Is this the most efficient or productive

EXHIBIT 11.2

THE ORIGINS OF UNHEALTHY CORPORATE CULTURES*

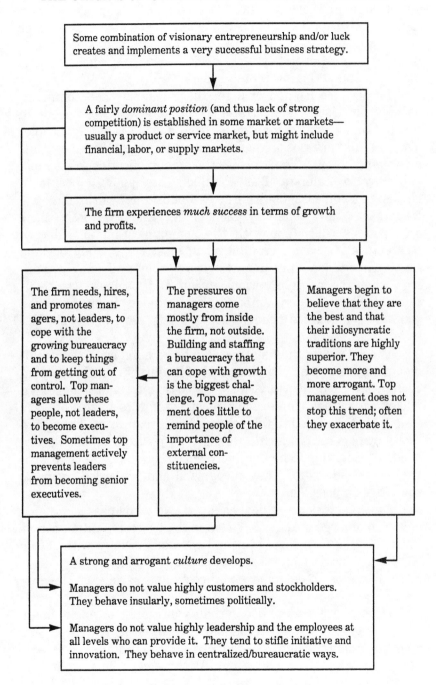

way to deliver those products and services? They gathered or led others to gather all the information necessary to answer those questions, including data from outsiders and people lower in the organization. They were decisive—making choices about direction and acting on those choices.

To produce needed change, these leaders then communicated their visions and strategies broadly in order to obtain understanding and commitment from a wide range of people. They used every possible opportunity to repeat key messages again and again. They made the communication as simple and easy to understand as possible. They allowed people to challenge the messages—thereby establishing healthy dialogue to replace static, one-way monologue. And they kept their own actions consistent with the communication in order to bolster the message's credibility; in most cases, they became living embodiments of the new cultures they desired. By aligning people to an appropriate vision and business strategy, these leaders helped empower like-minded managers who wanted to introduce needed changes but were being blocked by others.

These leaders then motivated a large number of their middle managers to play a similar kind of leadership role in creating change for their own divisions, departments, and groups. To make this happen, top executives stressed those parts of their visions that appealed to the values of their managers. They gave those managers as much autonomy as possible to enable the needed leadership. They actively encouraged attempts to provide that leadership. They recognized and rewarded as many successes as possible.

As a result, a great deal changed. New business strategies began to emerge that made sense in light of competitive conditions. New structures were implemented, usually with fewer hierarchical layers and less complexity. People began paying more attention to customers and costs and excellence. Performance improved.

When these leaders began their work, only a small number of people typically understood and agreed with what they were doing. But as their efforts produced positive results, their coalitions grew and grew over time. As these coalitions expanded, so did the new cultures, ones that better fit the firms' contexts and were better able to adapt to change (see exhibit 11.3). In

EXHIBIT 11.3

THE CREATION OF A PERFORMANCE-ENHANCING CULTURE*

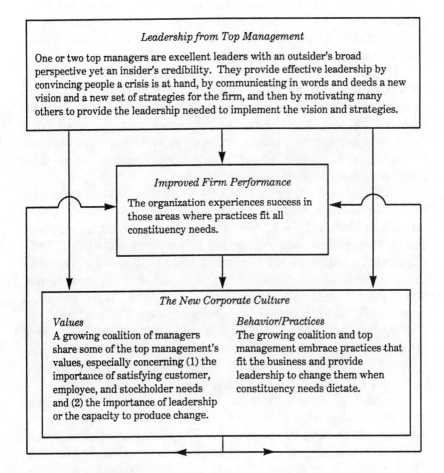

Leadership from Top Management

One or two top managers are excellent leaders with an outsider's broad perspective yet an insider's credibility. They provide effective leadership by convincing people a crisis is at hand, by communicating in words and deeds a new vision and a new set of strategies for the firm, and then by motivating many others to provide the leadership needed to implement the vision and strategies.

Improved Firm Performance

The organization experiences success in those areas where practices fit all constituency needs.

The New Corporate Culture

Values
A growing coalition of managers share some of the top management's values, especially concerning (1) the importance of satisfying customer, employee, and stockholder needs and (2) the importance of leadership or the capacity to produce change.

Behavior/Practices
The growing coalition and top management embrace practices that fit the business and provide leadership to change them when constituency needs dictate.

* This is a repeat of exhibit 8.7.

very large settings, the total time required for all this was significant: on the order of five to fifteen years.

The performance improvements that accompanied these cases of cultural change ranged from good to extraordinary. More important, people well acquainted with these cases seem to agree almost universally that the firms involved were left better positioned for the future.

*   *   *

The challenge for top management is different once a good culture has taken hold, but it is no less important.[1] Our research suggests that executives then need to cope with certain tensions and dilemmas. In a sense, the challenge is to orchestrate a difficult balancing act, the consequences of which determine whether a performance-enhancing culture is preserved or not.

Holding onto a good culture requires being both inflexible with regard to core adaptive values and yet flexible with regard to most practices and other values. It requires pushing hard to win, but not allowing the pride that comes with success to develop into arrogance. And it requires providing strong leadership, yet not strangling or smothering delicate leadership initiatives from below.

Our research suggests that two sets of actions can probably help with these dilemmas. In the first, executives need to differentiate basic values and behaviors that aid adaptation from the more specific practices needed to perform well today. This distinction needs to be made explicit when talking about culture. It also needs to be carefully noted in all written statements about culture and in all internal training courses. And it needs to be reflected and reinforced by specific actions. Without this distinction, practices of no long term significance can easily become important forces in a culture. Such practices can evolve into "sacred" traditions that ossify, resist change, and eventually undermine economic performance.

Second, although executives need to foster pride among employees, they also must be as intolerant as possible of arrogance in others and in themselves. They need to confront, and make others confront, as many of their failings as is practical. They need to create events where everyone in management is forced to listen to dissatisfied customers, angry stockholders, and alienated employees—not to embarrass or punish their managers, but to keep them informed and to help them realistically assess their strengths and weaknesses. And this must be done on an ongoing basis.

Both of these sets of actions, if taken to an extreme, will create serious problems. An emphasis only on adaptive values and behaviors can make it difficult to implement successfully today's strategies and tactics. Too much intolerance of arrogance coupled with a constant focus on problems can be depress-

EXHIBIT 11.4

PRESERVING PERFORMANCE-ENHANCING CULTURES

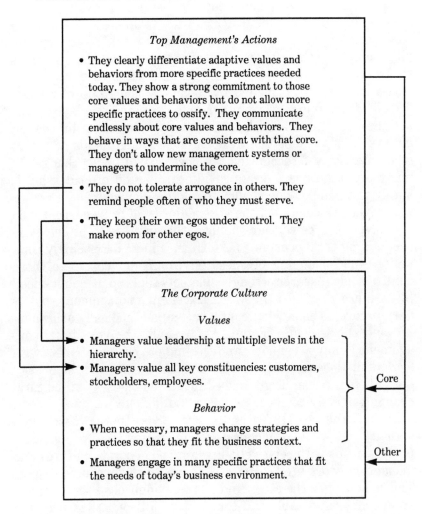

Top Management's Actions

- They clearly differentiate adaptive values and behaviors from more specific practices needed today. They show a strong commitment to those core values and behaviors but do not allow more specific practices to ossify. They communicate endlessly about core values and behaviors. They behave in ways that are consistent with that core. They don't allow new management systems or managers to undermine the core.

- They do not tolerate arrogance in others. They remind people often of who they must serve.

- They keep their own egos under control. They make room for other egos.

The Corporate Culture

Values

- Managers value leadership at multiple levels in the hierarchy.
- Managers value all key constituencies: customers, stockholders, employees.

Behavior

- When necessary, managers change strategies and practices so that they fit the business context.

- Managers engage in many specific practices that fit the needs of today's business environment.

Core

Other

ing and, ultimately, disempowering. The challenge is gaining the correct balance.

These actions are obviously not easy, but our research suggests they are both needed and feasible (see exhibit 11.4).

*   *   *

Ultimately, dozens, hundreds, or even thousands of managers became involved in important ways in the successful cultural change efforts that we studied—not only at the top, but at the middle and lower levels too. Without all this help, some of which typically came before a new CEO started providing strong leadership, and some of which may have influenced the CEO succession process, major cultural change would have been impossible. Nevertheless, excellent leadership from the top seems to be the essential ingredient in the cases we studied—leadership usually provided by a very small group of people. This leadership empowers other managers and employees who see the need for change but have been constrained by the old culture. It also helps win over the hearts and minds of others who have not yet recognized the necessity of major change. In many organizations today, providing this kind of leadership is surely the number one challenge for top management.

By our calculations, the vast majority of firms currently do not have cultures that are sufficiently adaptive to produce excellent long-term economic performance in an increasingly competitive and changing business environment. To create those cultures, our research strongly suggests that top managers need to do more than manage well. Excellent management, by its very nature, is somewhat conservative, methodically incremental, and short-term oriented. As a result, the very best management simply cannot produce major change. Only with leadership does one get the boldness, the vision, and the energy needed to create large and difficult changes—and cultural change certainly tends to be large and difficult.

Until the late 1970s and early 1980s, there was enough stability in a world of moderated competition (see exhibit 11.5) to allow firms with relatively unadaptive corporate cultures and managerially oriented corporate officers to survive and prosper. This is no longer the case. And all the evidence we see suggests an ever more unstable and competitive future, at least for the next decade.

The implications here are powerful—especially for those involved in executive staffing decisions and for aspiring executives everywhere. If our economic organizations are going to live up to their potential, we must find, develop, and encourage more people to lead in the service of others. Without leadership, firms cannot adapt to a fast moving world. But if leaders do not have the hearts of servants, there is only the potential for tyranny.

EXHIBIT 11.5

ENVIRONMENTAL STABILITY AND WORLD COMPETITION:
INDICES OF THE NEED FOR ADAPTIVE CORPORATE
CULTURES

Crude Oil Average Prices: A Stability Index
(Current Dollars per Barrel)

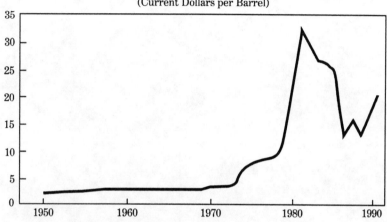

Source: Annual Energy Review.

Growth of World Trade (World Exports Plus Imports):
A Competitiveness Index
(In Billions of Dollars)

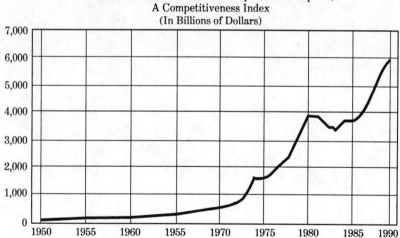

Source: International Monetary Fund.

APPENDIX

EXHIBIT A.1

THE FIRMS IN THE FIRST STUDY

Industry	Firms
Aerospace	Allied Signal, Boeing, General Dynamics, Lockheed, Martin Marietta, McDonnell Douglas, Northrop, Rockwell, Textron, United Technologies.
Airlines	American, Continental, Delta, Eastern, Northwest, PanAm, Piedmont, TWA, United, US Air
Apparel/Textiles	Hartmarx, Interco, Kellwood, Liz Claiborne, Manhattan, Oxford, Phillips Van Heusen, VF
Automotive	American Motors, Borg-Warner, Chrysler, Dana, Ford, Fruehauf, General Motors, Mack Truck, Navistar, Paccar
Banking	BankAmerica, Bankers Trust, Chase Manhattan, Chemical Bank, Citicorp, First Chicago, First Interstate, Manufacturers Hanover, J.P. Morgan, Security Pacific
Beverages	Anheuser-Busch, Brown-Forman, Coca-Cola, Coors, General Cinema, G. Heilman, PepsiCo, J. Seagram

(*Continued on next page*)

EXHIBIT A.1 (CONTINUED)

Chemicals	American Cyanamid, BASF, Celanese, Dow Chemical, Du Pont, FMC, W.R. Grace, Hercules, Monsanto, Union Carbide
Computers and Office Equipment	Apple Computer, Control Data, Digital Equipment, Hewlett-Packard, Honeywell, IBM, NCR, Pitney Bowes, Unisys, Wang Laboratories, Xerox
Food/Packaged Food	Archer Daniels Midland, Borden, ConAgra, CPC Industries, General Mills, IC Industries, Kraft, Pillsbury, Quaker Oats, Ralston Purina, Sara Lee
Forest/Products Paper	Boise Cascade, Champion, Georgia-Pacific, Great Northern Nekoosa, International Paper, Kimberly-Clark, Mead, Scott Paper, Weyerhaeuser
Life Insurance	Aetna Life & Casualty, Connecticut General, Equitable, John Hancock, Metropolitan Life, New York Life, Northwestern Mutual, Prudential, Teachers, Travelers
Petroleum Refining and Marketing	AMOCO, ARCO Chemical, Chevron, Exxon, Mobil, Phillips Petroleum, Shell Oil, Sun, Tenneco, Texaco, USX
Pharmaceuticals/Drugs	Abbott Laboratories, American Home Products, Baxter Travenol, Bristol-Myers Squibb, Johnson & Johnson, Eli Lilly, Merck, Pfizer, SmithKline

Printing/Publishing	R.R. Donnelley, Dow Jones, Gannett, Knight-Ridder, McGraw-Hill, New York Times, Time Inc., Times Mirror, Tribune Co., Washington Post
Retail/Food and Drug	Albertsons, American Stores, Great Atlantic & Pacific Tea (A&P), Kroger, Lucky Stores, Southland, Supermarkets General, Winn-Dixie Stores
Retail/Non–Food and Drug	Carter Hawley, Dayton Hudson, Federated Dept. Stores, K Mart, May Dept. Stores, J.C. Penney, Sears, Wal-Mart, Woolworth, Zayre
Rubber	Armstrong, Carlisle, Cooper Tire & Rubber, Dayco, Dorsey, Firestone, GenCorp, B.F. Goodrich, Goodyear Tire, Rubbermaid
Savings and Loan	H.F. Ahmanson, California Federal, Financial Corp. America, First Fed. Michigan, Gibraltar, Glendale, Golden West, Great Western, Home Federal, PSFS
Personal Care	Avon Products, Chesebrough Ponds, Clorox, Colgate-Palmolive, Economic Laboratories, Gillette, International Flavors & Fragrances, Lever Bros., Procter & Gamble, Revlon

(Continued on next page)

EXHIBIT A.1 (CONTINUED)

Textiles	Armstrong, Burlington, Collins & Aikman, DWG, Fieldcrest Cannon, Shaw Industries, Springs Industries, J.P. Stevens, United Merchants, W.P. Pepperell
Telecommunications	AT&T, American Information Technologies, Bell Atlantic, BellSouth, GTE, Nynex, Pacific Gas & Electric, Pacific Telesis Group, N.E. Telephone, S.W. Bell, US West

EXHIBIT A.2

THE METHODOLOGY USED TO CREATE STRENGTH-OF-CULTURE INDICES

We mailed the letter and questionnaire shown in exhibit A.3 to the top six officers in all 207 companies. That survey asked these executives about the strength of their competitors' corporate cultures (not their own) during the late 1970s and early 1980s. Our focus was on corporate or overall culture only, since none of the performance models described in Chapters 2 through 4 speak to the issue of subunit cultures. We chose late 1970s and early 1980s because a more recent period would not have allowed us to examine the impact of cultures on long-term economic performance and a more distant period would have posed additional problems for gathering valid data on those cultures.

To help respondents make a judgment about corporate culture, we told them that a strong culture was usually associated with affirmative answers to questions such as:

1. Have managers in competing firms commonly spoken of this company's "style" or way of doing things?
2. Has this firm both made its values known through a creed or credo and made a serious attempt to encourage managers to follow them?
3. Has the firm been managed according to long-standing policies and practices other than those of just the incumbent CEO?

Of the 600 people who replied to this inquiry (response rate of 48%), none argued with this definition and only three reported that it was too ambiguous to guide them in providing quantitative responses on a 1 (very strong culture) to 5 (very weak culture) scale.

With the information collected from the survey, we then constructed "culture strength indexes" by computing an average response for each firm. In five cases we chose not to do this either because many respondents said they did not know some competitor well or because their answers diverged too much. But indexes were successfully created in 202 cases. A complete list of these indices can be found in exhibit A.4.

To test the validity of these indices, we visited seven of the

202 firms and talked, this time, to insiders. The firms were: VF, ConAgra, Northwestern Mutual Life, Dow Chemical, J. C. Penney, McGraw-Hill, and First Chicago. At each company, the people we interviewed were asked the question about strength of culture for their own firm. Average responses were compared to the scores from the first survey. In all seven cases, the two numbers were very similar—the biggest variation was less than 20 percent.

We accepted these scores as credible for a variety of other reasons too. Exhibit A.4 tells us that 69 (or 34%) of the 207 firms had relatively strong cultures, with ratings in the first third of the range, that 103 had cultures of moderate strength, scoring in the middle of the range, and that only 30 had weak cultures. This overall profile is consistent with what we would expect from the corporate culture literature. Individual scores are also largely what we would expect based on that literature and on our knowledge of specific companies. The reader can examine exhibit 2.1 (and A.4) and draw his or her own conclusions about the validity of these indices.

EXHIBIT A.3

THE FIRST SURVEY

Page 1

Dear _____,

We need your assistance, for just one or two minutes, to help us select a sample of firms for a research project we are undertaking on the creation, maintenance, adaptation, and consequences (both good and bad) of a strong corporate culture.

Would you please rate firms competing in the _____ industry (not including your own) on the degree to which you feel their managers have been influenced in their decision making by a strong corporate culture? For purposes of the exercise, please associate a strong culture with affirmative responses to questions such as:

1. To what extent have managers in competing firms commonly spoken of a (company name) "style" or way of doing things?
2. To what extent has the firm both made its values known through a creed or credo and made a serious attempt to encourage managers to follow them? and
3. To what extent has the firm been managed according to longstanding policies and practices other than those of just the incumbent CEO?

Please rate the firms listed on the accompanying sheet on a scale of one to five, assigning a one to any firm you believe has a strong culture. Try to disassociate your ranking from the way in which these firms have performed in recent years.

Since a small sample of senior executives will be participating in this exercise, we would greatly appreciate your help. In return, we would be willing to provide you with the results of the exercise.

Sincerely,

(*Continued on next page*)

EXHIBIT A.3 (CONTINUED)
Page 2

	Circle 1 to designate the presence over the last decade of a strong corporate culture.				Circle 5 to designate the presence over the last decade of a very weak or nonexistent corporate culture.	Not Sure
Company A	1	2	3	4	5	NS
Company B	1	2	3	4	5	NS
Company C	1	2	3	4	5	NS
Company D	1	2	3	4	5	NS
Company E	1	2	3	4	5	NS
Company F	1	2	3	4	5	NS
Company G	1	2	3	4	5	NS
Company H	1	2	3	4	5	NS
Company I	1	2	3	4	5	NS

EXHIBIT A.4

STRENGTH OF CORPORATE CULTURE SCORES

1 = Strong corporate culture over the last decade

5 = Weak or nonexistent corporate culture over the last decade

1.	Wal-Mart	1.12	37.	Gannett	1.91
2.	J.P. Morgan	1.17	38.	Time Inc.	1.91
3.	Procter & Gamble	1.18	39.	ConAgra	1.91
4.	Northwestern M.L.	1.24	40.	Hewlett-Packard	1.93
5.	Dow Chemical	1.26	41.	Digital	1.93
6.	Shell Oil	1.30	42.	Coca-Cola	1.94
7.	Du Pont	1.32	43.	Golden West	1.95
8.	IBM	1.34	44.	J.C. Penney	1.95
9.	Delta	1.36	45.	Cooper Tire	2.00
10.	Boeing	1.38	46.	Shaw Industries	2.00
11.	Johnson & Johnson	1.39	47.	Apple Computers	2.06
12.	American Airlines	1.42	48.	Washington Post	2.14
13.	AT&T	1.42	49.	Int. F&F	2.14
14.	Ford	1.50	50.	Eli Lilly	2.16
15.	Citicorp	1.52	51.	BASF	2.18
16.	Merck	1.56	52.	Bell Atlantic	2.21
17.	Anheuser-Busch	1.63	53.	AMOCO	2.21
18.	Exxon	1.63	54.	Quaker Oats	2.21
19.	Dana	1.67	55.	Kroger	2.21
20.	Coors	1.67	56.	Sears	2.23
21.	H.F. Ahmanson	1.68	57.	May Dept. Stores	2.24
22.	Liz Claiborne	1.73	58.	So. NE Telephone	2.24
23.	PepsiCo	1.75	59.	R.R. Donnelley	2.25
24.	Goodyear	1.75	60.	S.W. Bell	2.25
25.	N.Y. Times	1.76	61.	Abbott Labs	2.26
26.	W.P. Pepperell	1.78	62.	Springs Industries	2.27
27.	VF	1.79	63.	Paccar	2.27
28.	Rubbermaid	1.80	64.	Martin Marietta	2.29
29.	General Motors	1.80	65.	Sara Lee	2.29
30.	Great Western	1.81	66.	Supermarkets Gen.	2.31
31.	Armstrong	1.82	67.	Bell South	2.32
32.	Dow Jones	1.83	68.	Home Federal	2.32
33.	Albertsons	1.86	69.	Pacific Telesis	2.33
34.	Kimberly Clark	1.86	70.	Prudential	2.35
35.	Bankers Trust	1.87	71.	Archer Daniels	2.35
36.	McDonnell Douglas	1.90	72.	Security Pacific	2.35

(Continued on next page)

EXHIBIT A.4 (CONTINUED)

73.	US Air	2.36	117.	Southland	2.82
74.	James River	2.36	118.	Brown-Forman	2.82
75.	Am. Home Prod.	2.38	119.	Chevron	2.83
76.	General Mills	2.38	120.	Colgate-Palmolive	2.84
77.	Pacific Gas	2.42	121.	Metropolitan Life	2.84
78.	Clorox	2.45	122.	Calif. Federal	2.86
79.	Dayton Hudson	2.45	123.	Scott Paper	2.86
80.	Collins & Aikman	2.45	124.	Burlington	2.88
81.	Lever Bros.	2.47	125.	Rockwell	2.89
82.	NYNEX	2.48	126.	Borden	2.91
83.	Northwest Airlines	2.48	127.	Monsanto	2.92
84.	Hartmarx	2.50	128.	NCR	2.95
85.	Mobil	2.52	129.	Woolworth	2.95
86.	Knight-Ridder	2.52	130.	Conn. General	2.96
87.	Piedmont	2.53	131.	J. Seagrams	3.00
88.	Xerox	2.55	132.	John Hancock	3.05
89.	Winn-Dixie Stores	2.56	133.	Champion	3.08
90.	ARCO	2.57	134.	Tribune	3.09
91.	Aetna	2.58	135.	Oxford	3.09
92.	Fieldcrest Cannon	2.59	136.	Chase Manhattan	3.09
93.	Texaco	2.60	137.	Hercules	3.10
94.	Weyerhaeuser	2.62	138.	Ralston Purina	3.10
95.	Gillette	2.64	139.	G.N. Nekoosa	3.10
96.	Glendale	2.65	140.	Phillips Petroleum	3.12
97.	K Mart	2.65	141.	Wang Labs	3.13
98.	Boise Cascade	2.65	142.	GTE	3.13
99.	U.S. West	2.65	143.	Mead	3.14
100.	Georgia Pacific	2.67	144.	GenCorp	3.15
101.	Lucky Stores	2.69	145.	American Stores	3.18
102.	Kraft	2.71	146.	United Tech.	3.19
103.	Borg-Warner	2.72	147.	Am. Cyanamid	3.20
104.	Lockheed	2.74	148.	Chesebrough Ponds	3.22
105.	Brist-Myers	2.74	149.	Sun Co.	3.28
106.	Chrysler	2.75	150.	First Interstate	3.28
107.	Pfizer	2.76	151.	Navistar	3.29
108.	Times-Mirror	2.77	152.	Baxter Travenol	3.30
109.	Mack Trucks	2.78	153.	Northrop	3.35
110.	Kellwood	2.80	154.	G. Heilman	3.38
111.	N.Y. Life	2.81	155.	General Dynamics	3.38
112.	J.P. Stevens	2.82	156.	McGraw-Hill	3.38
113.	Amer. Info. Tech.	2.82	157.	Celanese	3.39
114.	Travelers	2.82	158.	Allied Signal	3.44
115.	Avon	2.82	159.	Equitable Life	3.46
116.	United Airlines	2.82	160.	Chemical Bank	3.46

161.	CPC Industries	3.48	182.	USX	3.77
162.	Phillips VH	3.50	183.	Revlon	3.78
163.	Pillsbury	3.50	184.	First Chicago	3.80
164.	Control Data	3.54	185.	Zayre	3.81
165.	Interco	3.55	186.	Dayco	3.82
166.	Fed. Dept. Stores	3.56	187.	IC Industries	3.83
167.	Union Carbide	3.56	188.	International Paper	3.88
168.	B.F. Goodrich	3.57	189.	Firestone	3.93
169.	Armstrong	3.57	190.	Pitney Bowes	3.93
170.	FMC	3.59	191.	Honeywell	3.93
171.	SmithKline	3.59	192.	Gibraltar	3.95
172.	Manuf. Hanover	3.65	193.	Fruehauf	4.00
173.	W.R. Grace	3.67	194.	TWA	4.04
174.	Dorsey	3.67	195.	Unisys	4.08
175.	General Cinema	3.67	196.	PanAm	4.14
176.	A&P	3.69	197.	Carter Hawley	4.15
177.	PSFS	3.73	198.	United Merch.	4.18
178.	BankAmerica	3.73	199.	Eastern Airlines	4.30
179.	Tenneco	3.74	200.	Fin. Corp. Amer.	4.33
180.	Continental Airlines	3.76	201.	Manhattan Ind.	4.57
181.	Textron	3.77	202.	American Motors	4.63

EXHIBIT A.5

LONG-TERM ECONOMIC PERFORMANCE:
AN INDEX REPRESENTING NET INCOME GROWTH OVER
ELEVEN YEARS

1.	James River	169.7	39.	Brown Forman	29.4
2.	Wal-Mart	139.0	40.	Washington Post	28.8
3.	Phillips VH	113.4	41.	Security Pacific	28.3
4.	ConAgra	103.1	42.	Brist-Myers	28.1
5.	Piedmont	102.3	43.	Pfizer	28.1
6.	Wang Labs	80.2	44.	Archer Daniels	27.7
7.	Chrysler	75.0	45.	R.R. Donnelley	27.1
8.	US Air	61.8	46.	McGraw-Hill	26.4
9.	J. Seagrams	59.4	47.	Du Pont	25.6
10.	American Stores	55.4	48.	Chase Manhattan	24.9
11.	Digital	50.2	49.	Times Mirror	24.9
12.	SmithKline	48.8	50.	McDonnell Douglas	24.9
13.	Pitney Bowes	48.2	51.	J.P. Morgan	24.5
14.	Lockheed	45.6	52.	Time Inc.	24.4
15.	Bankers Trust	45.3	53.	United Tech.	24.2
16.	Anheuser-Busch	43.7	54.	Kraft	24.1
17.	Cooper Tire	43.0	55.	Springs Industries	24.0
18.	Hewlett-Packard	40.2	56.	Allied Signal	23.7
19.	VF	39.8	57.	NCR	23.6
20.	Golden West	39.2	58.	Eli Lilly	23.6
21.	Rockwell	39.1	59.	American Airlines	23.5
22.	General Cinema	37.3	60.	Clorox	23.3
23.	N.Y. Times	36.5	61.	General Dynamics	23.3
24.	Abbott Labs	35.8	62.	Johnson & Johnson	23.2
25.	Rubbermaid	35.7	63.	Hartmarx	22.4
26.	Zayre	34.7	64.	Am. Home Prod.	22.3
27.	Albertsons	34.1	65.	Quaker Oats	22.2
28.	Gannett	34.0	66.	PepsiCo	22.2
29.	Dow Jones	33.6	67.	Kroger	22.0
30.	United Airlines	32.5	68.	G.N. Nekoosa	21.9
31.	Dayton Hudson	32.1	69.	W.P. Pepperell	21.7
32.	G. Heilman	32.1	70.	Chemical Bank	21.7
33.	Hercules	31.6	71.	Collins & Aikman	21.5
34.	Boeing	31.4	72.	Celanese	21.5
35.	Sara Lee	30.8	73.	Coca-Cola	21.5
36.	May Dept. Stores	30.8	74.	So. NE Telephone	21.5
37.	Shaw	30.7	75.	Armstrong	21.4
38.	Baxter Travenol	29.5	76.	Knight-Ridder	21.3

77.	Merck	21.3	121.	Am. Cyanamid	14.6
78.	Kimberly-Clark	20.7	122.	Boise Cascade	14.5
79.	Shell Oil	20.7	123.	Dow Chemical	14.5
80.	Pacific Gas	20.7	124.	Champion	14.3
81.	Lucky Stores	20.7	125.	Aetna	14.3
82.	Martin Marietta	20.5	126.	Phillips Petroleum	13.7
83.	S.W. Bell	20.5	127.	Interco	13.7
84.	AMOCO	20.1	128.	BASF	13.6
85.	Exxon	19.0	129.	Textron	13.5
86.	Chesebrough Ponds	19.9	130.	Mead	13.2
87.	Delta	19.8	131.	Dana	13.2
88.	Mobil	19.8	132.	Fed. Dept. Stores	13.1
89.	Gillette	19.7	133.	Paccar	13.1
90.	Ralston Purina	19.2	134.	Xerox	13.1
91.	Scott Paper	19.2	135.	Weyerhaeuser	12.9
92.	IBM	19.1	136.	Tenneco	12.8
93.	Chevron	18.9	137.	Woolworth	12.6
94.	Int. F&F	18.4	138.	W.R. Grace	12.6
95.	Revlon	18.3	139.	H.F. Ahmanson	12.4
96.	Citicorp	18.2	140.	Kellwood	12.3
97.	Pillsbury	18.2	141.	Ford	12.0
98.	Supermarkets Gen.	17.8	142.	Monsanto	11.9
99.	Southland	17.8	143.	Oxford	11.6
100.	Borg-Warner	17.5	144.	Colgate-Palmolive	11.2
101.	ARCO	17.5	145.	Georgia Pacific	10.8
102.	CPC Industries	17.4	146.	First Chicago	10.7
103.	Sun Co.	17.2	147.	Northwest Airlines	10.3
104.	Great Western	17.1	148.	GenCorp	10.3
105.	Goodyear	17.0	149.	Honeywell	10.1
106.	IC Industries	16.8	150.	Texaco	9.9
107.	Borden	16.7	151.	General Motors	9.2
108.	Procter & Gamble	16.4	152.	Union Carbide	9.2
109.	Winn-Dixie Stores	16.4	153.	Coors	9.2
110.	FMC	16.3	154.	B.F. Goodrich	9.1
111.	J.C. Penney	16.0	155.	J.P. Stevens	8.5
112.	General Mills	15.8	156.	Fieldcrest Cannon	8.3
113.	Northrop	15.7	157.	AT&T	7.7
114.	GTE	15.6	158.	Dayco	7.7
115.	Manuf. Hanover	15.6	159.	Burlington	7.3
116.	K Mart	15.6	160.	Avon	7.0
117.	International Paper	15.5	161.	Carter Hawley	6.7
118.	First Interstate	15.2	162.	BankAmerica	5.8
119.	Sears	14.8	163.	Armstrong	5.3
120.	Travelers	14.7	164.	Firestone	4.4

(*Continued on next page*)

EXHIBIT A.5 (CONTINUED)

165.	Fruehauf	3.2	171.	Gibraltar	-3.7
166.	Mack Trucks	2.4	172.	Navistar	-13.4
167.	TWA	2.0	173.	Continental	-29.2
168.	Control Data	0.7	174.	Eastern Airlines	-86.1
169.	USX	0.1	175.	PanAm	-420.8
170.	Manhattan Ind.	-1.6			

This index was constructed by adding 1978 to 1988 net income and then dividing it by 1977 net, unless 1977 was an unusual year. If it was unusual, an average for the period 1975–1979 was used instead.

EXHIBIT A.6

LONG-TERM ECONOMIC PERFORMANCE:
AVERAGE RETURN ON INVESTED CAPITAL, 1977–1988

1.	Liz Claiborne	40.20	40.	Quaker Oats	14.39
2.	Am. Home Prod.	31.60	41.	Exxon	14.16
3.	Apple Computers	26.78	42.	CPC Industries	13.76
4.	SmithKline	24.76	43.	Knight-Ridder	13.68
5.	Dow Jones	24.64	44.	Ralston Purina	13.39
6.	Washington Post	21.97	45.	ConAgra	13.34
7.	Merck	21.44	46.	Revlon	13.21
8.	Abbott Labs	20.86	47.	Procter & Gamble	13.00
9.	Coca-Cola	20.65	48.	Digital	12.96
10.	Brist-Myers	20.53	49.	PepsiCo	12.95
11.	Int. F&F	20.16	50.	Kimberly Clark	12.76
12.	Eli Lilly	20.06	51.	NCR	12.66
13.	McGraw-Hill	19.76	52.	Albertsons	12.64
14.	VF	19.05	53.	Gillette	12.59
15.	Avon	18.94	54.	Anheuser-Busch	12.43
16.	IBM	18.81	55.	Aetna	12.35
17.	Wal-Mart	18.70	56.	Kraft	12.20
18.	Johnson & Johnson	17.89	57.	Lucky Stores	12.12
19.	G. Heilman	17.63	58.	AMOCO	12.10
20.	Rubbermaid	16.97	59.	General Cinema	11.98
21.	Boeing	16.75	60.	Time Inc.	11.98
22.	Winn-Dixie Stores	16.40	61.	Sara Lee	11.97
23.	Hewlett-Packard	16.35	62.	Collins & Aikman	11.66
24.	Gannett	16.04	63.	Ford	11.40
25.	General Mills	15.91	64.	McDonnell Douglas	11.30
26.	General Dynamics	15.90	65.	J.P. Morgan	11.26
27.	Martin Marietta	15.84	66.	FMC	11.18
28.	Clorox	15.70	67.	Hercules	11.00
29.	R.R. Donnelley	15.68	68.	Borg-Warner	10.89
30.	Pfizer	15.17	69.	Cooper Tire	10.83
31.	Paccar	15.17	70.	Phillips Petroleum	10.79
32.	Rockwell	15.01	71.	Colgate Palmolive	10.57
33.	Northrop	14.95	72.	Fed. Dept. Stores	10.42
34.	Times-Mirror	14.91	73.	Chevron	10.36
35.	Brown-Forman	14.68	74.	Armstrong	10.25
36.	Chesebrough Ponds	14.62	75.	Travelers	10.24
37.	N.Y. Times	14.51	76.	Shell Oil	10.13
38.	Lockheed	14.49	77.	United Tech.	10.09
39.	Pitney Bowes	14.40	78.	Dayton Hudson	10.09

(Continued on next page)

EXHIBIT A.6 (CONTINUED)

79.	May Dept. Stores	10.02	122.	Weyerhaeuser	7.22
80.	ARCO	9.98	123.	Sears	7.19
81.	Bankers Trust	9.84	124.	Chemical Bank	7.13
82.	Du Pont	9.83	125.	Phillips VH	7.12
83.	American Stores	9.81	126.	International Paper	7.09
84.	Borden	9.80	127.	Springs Industries	7.02
85.	Wang Labs	9.78	128.	First Interstate	6.91
86.	Archer Daniels	9.78	129.	Goodyear	6.72
87.	Dana	9.64	130.	Piedmont	6.69
88.	Shaw Industries	9.61	131.	Celanese	6.22
89.	Baxter Travenol	9.58	132.	Boise Cascade	6.20
90.	James River	9.36	133.	Chase Manhattan	6.16
91.	Supermarkets Gen.	9.28	134.	GenCorp	5.96
92.	Dow Chemical	9.27	135.	Champion	5.88
93.	Mobil	9.25	136.	Manuf. Hanover	5.74
94.	K Mart	9.19	137.	Pacific Gas	5.71
95.	Pillsbury	9.06	138.	Fieldcrest Cannon	5.64
96.	Am. Cyanamid	8.97	139.	First Chicago	5.55
97.	Oxford	8.96	140.	Union Carbide	5.52
98.	US Air	8.92	141.	Tenneco	5.38
99.	Woolworth	8.90	142.	Golden West	5.37
100.	J.C. Penney	8.90	143.	Texaco	5.36
101.	Xerox	8.86	144.	GTE	5.29
102.	G.N. Nekoosa	8.81	145.	Northwest Airlines	5.24
103.	Textron	8.78	146.	Citicorp	4.98
104.	Delta	8.78	147.	BankAmerica	4.97
105.	Interco	8.61	148.	W.R. Grace	4.97
106.	Hartmarx	8.60	149.	AT&T	4.78
107.	Sun Co.	8.44	150.	American Airlines	4.69
108.	Security Pacific	8.30	151.	Burlington	4.58
109.	J. Seagram	8.29	152.	Carter Hawley	4.56
110.	Mead	8.24	153.	H.F. Ahmanson	4.49
111.	Georgia Pacific	8.11	154.	Great Western	4.04
112.	Kroger	8.10	155.	United Airlines	3.65
113.	W.P. Pepperell	7.92	156.	J.P. Stevens	3.25
114.	Scott Paper	7.88	157.	B.F. Goodrich	2.52
115.	Allied Signal	7.71	158.	Manhattan Ind.	2.17
116.	Coors	7.69	159.	Gibraltar	2.07
117.	So. NE Tel.	7.48	160.	Firestone	1.51
118.	Kellwood	7.46	161.	Chrysler	1.43
119.	Monsanto	7.34	162.	Control Data	1.31
120.	Southland	7.32	163.	Fin. Corp. Amer.	1.26
121.	Honeywell	7.22	164.	USX	0.59

165.	A&P	-0.22	169.	United Merch.	-6.26
166.	Eastern Airlines	-0.44	170.	PanAm	-10.90
167.	Navistar	-2.36	171.	American Motors	-11.56
168.	Continental	-4.24			

EXHIBIT A.7

LONG-TERM ECONOMIC PERFORMANCE:
AVERAGE YEARLY INCREASES IN STOCK PRICES, 1977–1988

1.	Piedmont	57.04	40.	McGraw-Hill	18.57
2.	James River	47.48	41.	Security Pacific	18.53
3.	Wal-Mart	46.67	42.	W.P. Pepperell	18.52
4.	US Air	46.53	43.	Abbott Labs	18.48
5.	Liz Claiborne	40.71	44.	Brown-Forman	18.18
6.	Southland	39.07	45.	R.R. Donnelley	18.08
7.	ConAgra	35.65	46.	Brist-Myers	17.93
8.	Supermarkets Gen.	35.07	47.	Hewlett-Packard	17.50
9.	Wang Labs	33.08	48.	Dayton Hudson	17.35
10.	Cooper Tire	30.88	49.	Rockwell	17.29
11.	Apple Computers	30.06	50.	Pillsbury	17.26
12.	Albertsons	27.82	51.	Dow Jones	17.07
13.	Lockheed	27.37	52.	Sara Lee	16.19
14.	Pitney Bowes	25.68	53.	Great Western	16.84
15.	Collins & Aikman	25.06	54.	Merck	16.69
16.	Golden West	24.97	55.	Gannett	16.65
17.	Burlington	24.93	56.	Clorox	16.50
18.	G. Heilman	24.81	57.	Scott Paper	16.41
19.	VF	24.57	58.	Mead	15.19
20.	May Dept. Stores	24.16	59.	G.N. Nekoosa	15.80
21.	American Airlines	23.69	60.	Pfizer	15.73
22.	Anheuser-Busch	23.30	61.	Springs Industries	15.53
23.	N.Y. Times	22.98	62.	United Tech.	15.32
24.	Rubbermaid	22.90	63.	Times Mirror	15.27
25.	General Cinema	22.80	64.	Kellwood	15.17
26.	J. Seagram	22.56	65.	Kimberly-Clark	15.07
27.	Washington Post	22.46	66.	Shell Oil	14.96
28.	A&P	22.33	67.	United Airlines	14.88
29.	American Stores	21.67	68.	Borden	14.88
30.	Borg-Warner	21.35	69.	Celanese	14.86
31.	Shaw Industries	21.19	70.	Ford	14.82
32.	Chrysler	20.65	71.	Hartmarx	14.72
33.	Digital	20.65	72.	Eastern Airlines	14.69
34.	Boeing	20.45	73.	Eli Lilly	14.38
35.	Bankers Trust	20.43	74.	Phillips VH	14.38
36.	Quaker Oats	20.29	75.	Gillette	14.31
37.	Time Inc.	20.13	76.	General Dynamics	14.29
38.	Woolworth	18.73	77.	PepsiCo	14.10
39.	Archer Daniels	18.58	78.	B.F. Goodrich	14.00

79.	Northrop	13.52		121.	AMOCO	9.36
80.	SmithKline	13.46		122.	Travelers	9.28
81.	NCR	13.38		123.	Chase Manhattan	9.21
82.	Knight-Ridder	13.38		124.	Exxon	9.20
83.	So. NE Telephone	13.36		125.	ARCO	9.05
84.	Continental	13.31		126.	J.P. Stevens	9.03
85.	Allied Signal	13.06		127.	Textron	8.82
86.	J.P. Morgan	12.91		128.	Fin. Corp. Amer.	8.80
87.	Delta	12.90		129.	First Chicago	8.76
88.	H.F. Ahmanson	12.80		130.	K Mart	8.72
89.	Martin Marietta	12.69		131.	International Paper	8.66
90.	CPC Industries.	12.69		132.	First Interstate	8.58
91.	Paccar	12.63		133.	Goodyear	8.21
92.	Du Pont	12.25		134.	Chevron	8.12
93.	General Mills	12.25		135.	Dana	7.70
94.	Armstrong	12.19		136.	Int. F&F	7.58
95.	American Motors	12.06		137.	W.R. Grace	7.30
96.	Oxford	12.01		138.	Tenneco	7.08
97.	Coca-Cola	12.00		139.	Lucky Stores	6.77
98.	GTE	11.83		140.	Procter & Gamble	6.42
99.	Baxter Travenol	11.82		141.	Manhattan Ind.	6.56
100.	Champion	11.48		142.	Fieldcrest Cannon	6.40
101.	Dow Chemical	11.45		143.	Colgate-Palmolive	6.16
102.	Amer. Cyanamid	11.40		144.	Kroger	6.09
103.	Ralston Purina	11.31		145.	Sears	5.87
104.	Chemical Bank	11.27		146.	IBM	5.39
105.	Johnson & Johnson	11.02		147.	Winn-Dixie Stores	5.24
106.	Hercules	10.69		148.	Control Data	4.96
107.	Pacific Gas	10.67		149.	Navistar	4.94
108.	Fed. Dept. Stores	10.66		150.	Texaco	4.70
109.	J.C. Penney	10.65		151.	Xerox	4.35
110.	Northwest	10.65		152.	Coors	4.20
111.	Citicorp	10.30		153.	Sun Co.	4.15
112.	McDonnell Douglas	10.18		154.	FMC	3.99
113.	USX	10.02		155.	PanAm	3.96
114.	Am. Home Prod.	9.83		156.	Weyerhaeuser	3.54
115.	Mobil	9.72		157.	Manuf. Hanover	2.69
116.	Chesebrough Ponds	9.63		158.	Union Carbide	2.65
117.	Honeywell	9.52		159.	Georgia Pacific	1.67
118.	Boise Cascade	9.47		160.	Firestone	1.60
119.	Monsanto	9.42		161.	United Merch.	1.24
120.	Aetna	9.40		162.	GenCorp	0.77

(*Continued on next page*)

EXHIBIT A.7 (CONTINUED)

163.	Phillips Petroleum	0.07	168.	Gibraltar	−11.87
164.	BankAmerica	−0.18	169.	Interco	−12.04
165.	AT&T	−2.15	170.	Kraft	−57.35
166.	Carter Hawley	−3.72	171.	Revlon	−71.52
167.	Avon	−8.51			

EXHIBIT A.8A

CULTURE STRENGTH AND NET INCOME GROWTH*

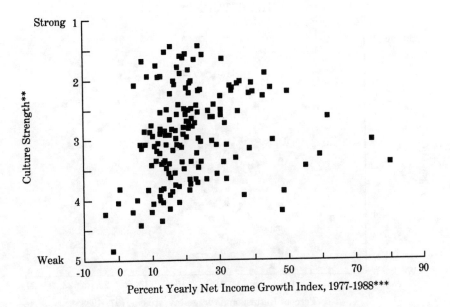

* Ten firms had net income growth indices above 90 or below −10 and are not shown.
** See exhibits A.3 and A.4.
*** See exhibit A.5.

EXHIBIT A.8B

CULTURE STRENGTH AND RETURN ON AVERAGE INVESTMENT*

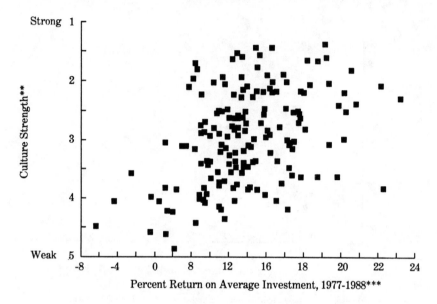

* Four firms had returns above 28 percent or below −8 percent and are not shown.
** See exhibits A.3 and A.4.
*** See exhibit A.6.

EXHIBIT A.9

THE SECOND STUDY:
THE STRONGER PERFORMERS

	Culture Score	Index of Net Income Growth	1977 Revenues (In billions)	1988 Revenues (In billions)	1977 Stock Price	1988 Stock Price	Number of Employees In 1977 (In thousands)	Number of Employees in 1988 (In thousands)
American Airlines	1.42	23.5	$2.30	$8.80	$12½	$51	32.0	68.0
Bankers Trust	1.87	45.3	1.45	2.70	9	35	12.5	12.7
Anheuser-Busch	1.63	43.7	1.84	9.70	3½	32	14.0	41.0
PepsiCo	1.75	22.2	3.55	13.00	9	39½	76.0	235.0
Hewlett-Packard	1.93	40.2	1.36	9.80	10	48	35.0	87.0
ConAgra	1.91	103.1	.54	9.50	2	28	6.0	43.0
Shell	1.30	20.7	26.05	47.04	14	57	93.0	80.0
Albertson's	1.86	34.1	1.80	6.80	4	37½	20.4	50.0
Dayton Hudson	2.45	32.1	2.17	12.20	9½	41½	59.0	135.0
Wal-Mart	1.12	139.0	.68	20.60	½	31	13.5	220.0
Golden West	1.95	39.2	.21	1.38	4½	31	1.0	3.2
Springs	2.27	24.0	.68	1.80	8⅜	32¾	19.7	23.3
Median	1.89	36.7	1.63	9.60	8.7	36¼	20.10	59.0
Mean	1.79	47.3	3.55	11.90	7.2	38.7	31.8	83.2

EXHIBIT A.10

THE SECOND STUDY: THE WEAKER PERFORMERS

	Culture Score	Index of Net Income Growth	1977 Revenues (In billions)	1988 Revenues (In billions)	1977 Stock Price	1988 Stock Price	Number of Employees in 1977 (In thousands)	Number of Employees in 1988 (In thousands)
Northwest	2.48	10.3	$1.00	$5.65	$26½	$53	11.4	35.5
Citicorp	1.52	18.2	5.05	13.00	12½	25⅞	47.0	90.0
Coors	1.67	9.2	.59	1.52	14¾	18½	8.2	10.5
Xerox	2.55	13.1	5.08	11.50	51	57	48.8	113.0
Archer Daniels	2.35	27.7	2.11	6.80	4¾	26⅜	5.0	9.0
Texaco	2.60	9.9	27.90	35.00	26¼	48¾	70.6	41.8
Winn-Dixie	2.56	16.4	4.00	9.00	17½	44	51.0	83.8
J.C. Penney	1.95	16.0	9.37	14.80	18⅔	52½	193.0	190.0
H.F. Ahmanson	1.68	12.4	.86	3.50	6½	16½	3.8	11.6
Fieldcrest Cannon	2.59	8.3	.42	1.34	13	22	12.4	22.0
Median	2.42	12.8	3.06	7.90	16.13	35.19	29.7	38.7
Mean	2.20	14.2	5.64	10.21	19.14	36.45	45.1	60.6

EXHIBIT A.11

THE SECOND SURVEY

The Solicitation Letter to Financial Analysts

Dear

We need just a few minutes of your time to help us with our research on corporate culture—more specifically, on what if any relationship exists between the overall culture of firms and their long-term economic performance. Our study, which began in 1987, has thus far included a survey of the top six executives in 200 corporations, field visits to seven of those firms, an economic analysis of all 200 companies, and an in-depth historical examination of a select few.

In this stage of our work, we are focusing on 24 firms, two of which you probably know well. Sometime soon our research assistant, James Leahey, will call to see if he can set up a brief appointment with you. We would be very appreciative if you could see him. In return, we would be happy to send you an early draft of our report on this project.

With best regards,
James L. Heskett
John P. Kotter

Interview Guide (interviews were tape recorded)

1. What words or phrases best describe the corporate culture at (Company) during the last 15 years? (If it has changed much in the past 15 years, describe what has changed and what has remained constant.)

2. Has the culture helped the firm's performance over the past dozen years? Or hurt it? Or both? Or neither? _____helped, _____hurt, _____both, _____neither. How has it helped or hurt?

3. If part of the culture helped or hurt the firm's performance, how did the culture get to be this way?

4. How much has the culture at (Company) valued customers? Has there been a deep-seated belief, widely shared in this

firm, that they should try to achieve some standard of excellence in serving the interests of customers?

1	2	3	4	5	6	7
Definitely Not		Minimally Yes		Partially Yes		Absolutely Yes

5. How much has the culture at (Company) valued employees? Has there been a deep-seated belief, widely shared in the firm, that they should try to achieve some standard of excellence in serving the interests of employees?

1	2	3	4	5	6	7
Definitely Not		Minimally Yes		Partially Yes		Absolutely Yes

6. How much has the culture at (Company) valued stockholders? Has there been a deep-seated belief, widely shared in the firm, that they should try to achieve some standard of excellence in serving the interests of stockholders?

1	2	3	4	5	6	7
Definitely Not		Minimally Yes		Partially Yes		Absolutely Yes

7. How much has the culture at (Company) valued excellent leadership from its managers? Has there been a deep-seated belief, widely shared in the firm, that they should aggressively seek people with leadership potential, develop that potential, and then encourage people to lead?

1	2	3	4	5	6	7
Definitely Not		Minimally Yes		Partially Yes		Absolutely Yes

8. How well has the culture at (Company) fit the market, competitive, technological, and other environments in which the firm has found itself? (Note: If it fit well at one time, but no longer does [or vice versa], circle two numbers, date each, and describe below the story behind this.)

1	2	3	4	5	6	7
Terribly		Not Well		Well		Superbly

EXHIBIT A.12

THE SECOND STUDY:
INTERVIEW GUIDE FOR DISCUSSIONS WITH MANAGERS

---

1. How much has the corporate culture at your firm changed in the last 15 years?

2. What has specifically changed?

3. What hasn't changed?

4. Why has your culture changed (so much or so little)?

5. For parts that changed, how did that happen?

6. How easily did those changes occur?

7. For those parts that didn't change, why did they perpetuate themselves? How?

8. What is the history of your culture?

9. When and how did the current culture first appear?

10. Has your culture either helped or hurt your economic performance over the past 15 years? Why and how?

THE FIRMS IN THE THIRD STUDY

COMPANY NAME	1977 Sales (millions)	1988 Sales (millions)	1977 Employees (thousands)	1988 Employees (thousands)	1977 Stock Price Close	1988 Stock Price Close	1977 Net Income (millions)	1988 Net Income (millions)	1977–88 Sales Growth(%)	1977–88 Employee Growth(%)	1977–88 Stock Price Growth(%)	1977–88 Net Inc. Growth(%)
Adolph Coors	593	1,522	8.2	10.5	13.25	20.00	67.7	46.9	159	29	51	-31
H.F. Ahmanson	865	3,515	3.8	11.6	6.29	16.38	103.7	202.0	306	209	160	95
Avon Products	1,648	3,063	27.3	28.4	48.13	19.50	191.5	-404.5	86	4	-60	-311
BankAmerica	5,425	10,181	72.9	61.0	22.88	17.63	396.3	728.0	88	-16	-23	83
Citicorp	5,516	32,024	47.2	89.0	11.44	25.88	373.8	1,858.0	481	89	126	397
Ford Motor Co.	37,842	92,446	479.3	358.9	10.17	50.50	1,672.8	5,300.2	144	-25	397	217
Fieldcrest Cannon	417	1,338	12.4	22.0	14.13	19.88	17.3	11.3	221	77	41	-35
First Chicago	1,489	4,816	8.6	16.1	18.50	29.63	114.1	513.1	223	87	60	350
General Motors	54,961	12,186	797.0	765.7	31.44	41.75	3,337.5	4,858.3	122	-4	33	45
Goodyear	6,628	10,810	152.5	113.7	17.25	51.13	205.8	350.1	63	-25	196	70
J.C. Penney	9,369	15,296	193.0	190.0	17.75	50.63	295.0	807.0	63	-2	185	174
K Mart	10,064	27,550	208.5	350.0	18.25	35.13	302.9	803.0	174	68	93	165
Kroger	6,748	19,053	60.6	160.0	6.91	8.88	60.6	34.5	182	164	28	-43

Navistar International	5,975	4,080	93.2	15.72	30.25	5.38	203.7	244.0	−32	−88	−82	20
NWA	1,046	5,650	11.4	35.53	23.63	51.75	92.7	135.1	440	211	119	46
PanAm	1,907	3,569	NA	24.61	5.00	2.25	45.0	−72.7	87	−23	−55	−262
Sears	17,224	50,251	460.0	520.00	28.00	40.88	838.0	1,453.7	192	13	46	74
Eastern	2,036	3,806	34.3	30.27	6.13	NA	34.7	−335.4	87	−12	51	−1,065
Texaco	27,921	33,544	70.6	41.82	27.75	51.13	930.8	1,304.0	21	−41	84	40
Xerox	5,077	15,994	104.0	113.25	46.75	58.38	406.6	388.0	215	9	25	−5
Average									166%	36%	74%	1%

NOTES

PREFACE

1. See *The Leadership Factor* (New York: Free Press, 1988); and *A Force for Change: How Leadership Differs from Management* (New York: Free Press, 1990).
2. See *The Leadership Factor*, chap. 8; and *A Force for Change*, chap. 10.
3. The course is called "Management Policy and Practice" and is taught in the fall of their second year.

1. THE POWER OF CULTURE

1. The first known publication to have "culture" in its title is Edward B. Tylor, *Primitive Culture: Researches into the Development of Mythology, Philosophy, Religion, Art, and Custom*, 2 vols. (New York: Henry Holt, 1887).
2. Franz Boas, "The Central Eskimo," Bureau of Ethnology Annual Report No. 6, pp. 399–664 (Washington, D.C.: Smithsonian Institution, 1884); Bronislaw Malinowski, *Argonauts of the Western*

Pacific: An Account of Native Enterprise and Adventure in the Archipelagoes of Melanesian New Guinea (London: George Routledge & Sons, 1922); A. R. Radcliffe-Brown, "The Mother's Brother in South Africa," *South African Journal of Science* 21 (1924): 542–555; and Ruth Benedict, *Patterns of Culture* (Boston: Houghton Mifflin, 1934).

3. The word "culture" is used with many different meanings in everyday conversation and in scholarly literature. The definition we employ, shown in exhibit 1.1, is closely related to Edgar Schein's in his *Organizational Culture and Leadership* (San Francisco: Jossey-Bass, 1985).

4. See Kotter, *A Force For Change*, chap. 3.

5. See, for example, John P. Kotter, Leonard Schlesinger, and Vijay Sathe, *Organization: Text, Cases, and Readings on the Management of Organization Design and Change*, 2d ed. (Homewood, Ill.: Richard D. Irwin, 1986).

6. Meryl Louis is the one writer who has made this point most clearly. See her "Sourcing Workplace Cultures: Why, When, and How," in Kilmann, Saxton, and Serpa, eds., *Gaining Control of the Corporate Culture* (San Francisco: Jossey-Bass, 1986), pp. 126–136.

7. Schein's discussion of this in *Organizational Culture and Leadership* is most thorough. See also Gordon Donaldson and Jay Lorsch, *Decision Making at the Top* (New York: Basic Books, 1983); and Alan L. Wilkins and Kerry J. Patterson, "You Can't Get There from Here: What Will Make Cultural Change Projects Fail," in Kilman, Saxton, and Serpa, eds., *Gaining Control of the Corporate Culture*, pp. 262–291.

8. All the early books on corporate culture make this point. See the discussion in Donaldson and Lorsch, *Decision Making at the Top*.

9. See Kotter, *A Force for Change*.

10. See Tom Peters and R. H. Waterman, *In Search of Excellence* (New York: Harper & Row, 1982); and Schein, *Organizational Culture and Leadership*.

11. See Vijay Sathe's discussion of this in *Culture and Related Corporate Realties* (Homewood, Ill.: Richard D. Irwin, 1985), and the article in his book by John Van Manenn, "People Processing: Strategies of Organizational Socialization" pp. 223–243.

12. See Bill Ouchi, *Theory Z* (Reading, Mass.: Addison-Wesley, 1981); Peters and Waterman, *In Search of Excellence*, Richard T. Pascale and Anthony G. Athos, *The Art of Japanese Management* (New York: Simon & Schuster, 1981); Terry E. Deal and Allan A. Kennedy, *Corporate Cultures* (Reading, Mass.: Addison-Wesley, 1982).

13. See Peters and Waterman, *In Search of Excellence;* and Schein, *Organizational Culture and Leadership.*
14. See Deal and Kennedy, *Corporate Cultures;* and Schein, *Organizational Culture and Leadership.*
15. See Deal and Kennedy, *Corporate Cultures.*
16. See Donaldson and Lorsch, *Decision Making at the Top.*
17. See Schein, *Organizational Culture and Leadership.*
18. See Donaldson and Lorsch, *Decision Making at the Top;* and Schein, *Organizational Culture and Leadership.*
19. See Schein, *Organizational Culture and Leadership;* and Sathe, *Culture and Related Corporate Realities.*
20. See Sathe, *Culture and Related Corporate Realities.*
21. See Fritz J. Roethlisberger and William J. Dickson, *Management and the Worker: An Account of a Research Program Conducted by the Western Electric Company, Hawthorne Works, Chicago* (Cambridge: Harvard University Press, 1939).
22. The phrase "corporate" or "organizational culture" does not appear in James G. March's *Handbook of Organizations* (Chicago: Rand McNally, 1965); or in Peter Drucker's *Management: Tasks, Responsibilities, Practices* (New York: Harper & Row, 1974). Even the word "culture" is hard to find in organizational literature, although some of the ideas we now associate with this concept were developed under the heading of "norms and values in small groups." A classic example would be George Homans, *The Human Group* (New York: Harcourt, Brace & World, 1950). The first scholarly work to focus on organizational culture appeared in 1979. See Andrew Pettigrew's "On Studying Organizational Culture," *Administrative Science Quarterly* 24 (1979): 570–581.
23. These include Anthony Athos (who had associations with Harvard and McKinsey), Stanley Davis (Harvard, MAC), Terry Deal (Harvard), Allan Kennedy (McKinsey), Jay Lorsch (Harvard, MAC), Joanne Martin (Stanford, Harvard), Bill Ouchi (Stanford), Richard Pascale (Stanford, Harvard), Tom Peters (McKinsey, Stanford), and Edgar Schein (MIT, MAC). It is probably not a coincidence that the two most centrally involved organizations— McKinsey and Harvard Business School—both have strong cultures.
24. In particular, we are thinking of work by Ouchi and Pascale.
25. Work by Peters, Waterman, Deal, Kennedy, Donaldson, and Lorsch.
26. Such as Stan Davis's *Managing Corporate Culture* (Cambridge, Mass.: Ballinger, 1984); and Donaldson and Lorsch's *Decision Making at the Top.*

27. A poll reported in the *Wall Street Journal* in 1989 said that 80 percent of senior human resource managers felt their firm's cultures needed to be changed and that many of them were trying to do just that.

28. *Time*, 24 July 1989, p. 35.

29. See, for example, Kilmann, Saxton, and Serpa, eds., *Gaining Control of Corporate Culture*.

30. Joanne Martin at Stanford has probably been the most intelligent critic of the popular books on culture, including simplistic performance theories. See Caren Siehl and Joanne Martin, "Organizational Culture: A Key to Financial Performance?" in Benjamin Schneider, ed., *Organizational Climate and Culture*, pp. 241–281 (San Francisco: Jossey-Bass, 1990).

31. See Alan Wilkins, *Developing Corporate Character* (San Francisco: Jossey-Bass, 1989).

32. For example, see Thomas Fitzgerald, "Can Change in Organizational Culture Really Be Managed?" *Organizational Dynamics* 17, no. 2 (Autumn 1988): 4.

33. We also began with a commitment to using multiple methods, not just "soft" or "hard" approaches. See Denise Rousseau's discussion of these issues in "Assessing Organizational Culture: The Case for Multiple Methods," in Schneider, ed., *Organizational Climate and Culture*, pp. 153–192.

2. STRONG CULTURES

1. This seems to have been first stated by Geert Hofstede in his *Culture's Consequences* (Beverly Hills, Calif.: Sage, 1980), p. 394; although it is implied in Philip Selznick's earlier work, *Leadership in Administration* (New York: Harper & Row, 1957).

2. *Corporate Cultures*, pp. 8–13.

3. Ibid., p. 9. Deal and Kennedy report that Tandem's turnover rate is one-third the national average for the computer industry.

4. "A Business and Its Beliefs," McKinsey Foundation Lecture, New York: McGraw–Hill, 1963.

5. For example: *Fortune* reported a survey of 305 CEOs in which "all but a handful think strong corporate values are important to their companies' success" (17 October 1983, p. 66).

6. Warren Bennis, speaking on culture in 1985, summarized his understanding of these books by saying, "Strong culture seems to be a driving force behind successful companies." This statement can be found in *Corporate Culture and Change*, a Conference Board Report, NY: 1986, p. 63.

7. Margaret H. Beyer, *The Role of Corporate Cultures in the Management of High-Performing Banks* (Newark: University of Delaware, June 1988), p. 4.

8. See Ed Schein's discussion of this in *Organizational Culture and Leadership*.

9. See Kilmann, Saxton, and Serpa, eds., *Gaining Control of the Corporate Culture*, p. 4.

10. Richard Boyatzis, for one, has discussed how this can happen: A mythology develops in the strong culture about the competencies of high-performing managers and then promotion decisions are based on this, even when the mythology is wrong. Those managers then lead people in the wrong direction. See the first two chapters of *The Competent Manager* (New York: John Wiley & Sons, 1982).

11. *The Art of Japanese Management*, p. 197.

12. *In Search of Excellence*, p. 103.

13. See Kotter's discussion of this in *A Force for Change*.

14. We used industry groupings found in *Fortune* and *Business Week*. We restricted ourselves in this first study to the U.S. market for reasons of convenience of access.

15. By using a culture strength index for the "late '70s and early '80s" and a performance index for 1977–1988, we allowed for the possibility of a one- to three-year lag effect. See Daniel Denison, *Corporate Culture and Organizational Effectiveness* (New York: John Wiley & Sons, 1990).

16. The correlation coefficients are $+0.26$ (culture strength and market value growth), $+0.46$ (culture strength and net income growth), and $+0.31$ (culture strength and return on average investment). The industry adjusted coefficients are virtually the same: $+0.26$, $+0.42$, and $+0.30$. These correlations are not modest by most social science standards, but they are in the case of a one-factor theory (where one factor is posited to strongly determine another).

17. See Maryann Keller, *Rude Awakening* (New York: William Morrow, 1989).

18. See Donald R. Katz, *The Big Store* (New York: Viking Penguin, 1987).

19. See "The 10 Worst-Managed Companies in America," *Financial World*, 6 October 1987, pp. 30–40.

20. See Jonathan Hicks, "For Goodyear Chief, the Heat is On," *The New York Times*, 21 January 1989, p. 37.

21. See *A Force for Change*, chap. 7; also, Andrew Tanzer, "They Didn't Listen to Anybody," *Forbes*, 15 December 1986, pp. 168–169.

22. *The Wall Street Journal*, 22 September 1989, Section B, p. 1, col. 3.
23. See Robert Hutchinson, *Off the Books* (New York: William Morrow, 1986).
24. See Harold van B. Cleveland and Thomas F. Huertas, *Citibank 1812–1970* (Cambridge, Mass.: Harvard University Press, 1985).
25. We used the business diversity measures in the Compustat data base. The correlation coefficient was −0.152.

3. STRATEGICALLY APPROPRIATE CULTURES

1. Almost everyone writing on this topic supports "fit" theory in passing, but few make it the center of their ideas. Schein, Lorsch, and Davis seem to have leaned toward this model the most. One could argue that this whole perspective comes from early work by Lorsch (see Paul Lawrence and Jay Lorsch, *Organization and Environment* [Boston: Harvard Business School Press, 1967]); or even earlier work by Tom Burns and G. M. Stalker (see *The Management of Innovation* [London: Tavistock, 1961]).
2. See George G. Gordon, "The Relationship of Corporate Culture to Industry Sector and Corporate Performance," in Kilmann, Saxton and Serpa, eds., *Gaining Control of the Corporate Culture*, pp. 103–125.
3. Reported in *Decision Making at the Top*.
4. They use the term "belief system" instead of cultures.
5. *Decision Making at the Top*, p. 151.
6. Based on interviews we have conducted.
7. To avoid the problem in earlier culture studies of false positive findings due to a lack of comparative research (matched good and bad cases) and/or an unusual set of industries (e.g., too much high-tech), we used the following criteria to select that sample: (1) the industries included had to be a diverse lot, (2) all firms had to have relatively similar strength of corporate culture scores, (3) half the companies had to have performance scores much higher than the other half, (4) the better and worse performers had to be matched by industry and, if possible, in other potentially relevant ways, and (5) all of the firms had to be "normal" or at least not highly idiosyncratic in a potentially relevant way—no founders still acting as CEOs, no especially large or small firms. In general, we succeeded in implementing these criteria, although the industry matches were far from perfect in a few cases (e.g., HP versus Xerox).

8. Whenever possible, we selected analysts chosen by *Institutional Investor* magazine as the best in their fields.

9. We visited Albertson's, American Airlines, Anheuser-Busch, Bankers Trust, Conagra, Coors, Dayton Hudson, Golden West, Hewlett-Packard, J. C. Penney, Shell, Springs, and Texaco. We also interviewed managers from Citicorp, Northwest, Pepsico, and Xerox as opportunities to do so arose.

10. Rejection of the negative-correlation theory is also supported by the data in exhibits 2.1 and A.8.

4. ADAPTIVE CULTURES

1. This perspective is derived from many different antecedents. Theory III is closely related to the "organizational development" literature (for example, work by Richard Beckhard, *Organization Development* [Reading, Mass.: Addison-Wesley, 1969]; and Michael Beer, *Organization Change and Development* [Glenview, Ill.: Scott Foresman, 1980]). It is also closely related to the work coming out of the University of Michigan (see Rensis Likert, *The Human Organization* [New York: McGraw–Hill, 1967]; and, more recently, Denison, *Corporate Culture and Organizational Effectiveness*).

2. Kilmann, Saxton, and Serpa, *Gaining Control of the Corporate Culture*, p. 356.

3. *The Change Masters* (New York: Simon & Schuster, 1983).

4. See *A Force for Change.*

5. See Peters and Waterman, *In Search of Excellence*, and Tom Peters and Nancy Austin, *A Passion for Excellence; The Leadership Difference* (New York: Random House, 1985).

6. See *A Force for Change.*

7. See Chapter 3, n. 9.

8. Rather than promote conformity, these executives encourage something similar to what Schein has called "creative individualism"—adherence to pivotal values and norms but rejection of others. See his "Organizational Socialization and the Profession of Management," *Industrial Management Review* 9 (1968): 1–15.

5. THE CASE OF HEWLETT-PACKARD

1. Examples of this phenomenon are discussed in Kotter, *The Leadership Factor*, chaps. 4, 5, and 6.

2. Information on Hewlett-Packard comes from interviews with managers conducted by Kotter in July 1990 and from company documents.
3. Interview with Kotter, July 1990.
4. Interview with Kotter, July 1990.
5. Interview with Kotter, July 1990.
6. Interview with Kotter and Heskett, 1 August 1990.
7. Interview with Kotter, June 1990.

6. THE NATURE OF LOW-PERFORMANCE CULTURES

1. The information we collected for this inquiry comes from three sources: (1) our second study (a group of eight firms were in both studies), (2) publicly available sources (mostly books and articles), and (3) earlier personal contact with five of these firms.
2. This distinction is made in Kotter, *A Force for Change*, chap. 1.
3. Reported to Heskett in interviews with Texaco management, January 1991.
4. Reported to Heskett in interviews with Coors management, January 1991.
5. See, for example, J. P. Wright, *On a Clear Day You Can See General Motors* (Grosse Pointe, Mich.: Wright Enterprises, 1979).
6. This historical material on Xerox comes from interviews with current and former Xerox employees, company publications, and John H. Dessauer, *My Years with Xerox* (Garden City, N.Y.: Doubleday, 1971); Gary Jacobson and John Hillkirk, *Xerox: American Samurai* (New York: Macmillan, 1986); and Douglas K. Smith and Robert C. Alexander, *Fumbling the Future* (New York: William Morrow, 1988).
7. Dessauer, *My Years with Xerox*, pp. 4, 60, 88, 203, 204.
8. Smith and Alexander, *Fumbling the Future*, p. 129.
9. Dessauer, *My Years with Xerox*, pp. 136, 142, 147.
10. Smith and Alexander, *Fumbling the Future*, p. 48.
11. Ibid., page 156.
12. Ibid., page 181.
13. Ibid., page 181.
14. The executive hired by Xerox to help get them into computers says he was not consulted regarding the purchase of SDS.
15. Ibid., page 134.
16. Ibid., pp. 135–141.
17. Ibid., page 176.
18. Ibid., page 221.
19. *Xerox: American Samurai*, p. 3.

20. We estimate that only 5%–10% of the 207 firms in our original study had corporate cultures that significantly enhanced economic performance.
21. There appears to be plenty of support for this conclusion. See, for example, Todd Jick's "The Challenge of Change," Harvard Business School Note No. 490-016.
22. There is a considerable body of work in psychology that shows that values do not change easily. Here, they can become an obstacle to cultural change.
23. A. M. Pettigrew has written persuasively about this issue. See, for example, his "Conclusion: Organizational Climate and Culture: Two Constructs in Search of a Role," in Schneider, *Organizational Climate and Culture*, pp. 413–433.

7. PEOPLE WHO CREATE SUCCESSFUL CHANGE

1. Pascale and Athos and Peters and Waterman avoided the subject. Davis, Deal and Kennedy, and Ouchi all offered prescriptions for cultural change. After talking to firms who tried to implement their ideas, we have found that these prescriptions haven't been very effective.
2. *Developing Corporate Character*, pp. xi, xii.
3. As early as 1983, *Fortune* did a "review of the evidence" and reached a similar conclusion. See Brouttal, "The Corporate Culture Vultures," *Fortune*, 17 October 1983, pp. 66–72.
4. Data on cultural changes at these ten firms came mostly from work already completed by Kotter. The TRS, ConAgra, and SAS cases were researched in conjunction with his book *A Force for Change*. The British Airways, GE, ICI, and Xerox cases had been documented for teaching purposes at Harvard. Bankers Trust, First Chicago, and Nissan were then studied specifically for this project. The authors visited each of these firms. In two of the three cases, Kotter talked extensively with managers and executives about their corporate cultures, about what had changed over the past ten to fifteen years, and about what had created that change.
5. We also found other firms in the process of making significant efforts to change their cultures (e.g., Texaco, Coors), but it is too early to determine how successful they will be.
6. Others have stated or implied similar conclusions. See Noel M. Tichy and Mary Anne Devanna, *The Transformational Leader* (New York: John Wiley & Sons, 1986); and Schein, *Organizational Culture and Leadership*.

7. For a discussion of the differences between management and leadership, see Kotter, *A Force for Change.*

8. Others have made similar observations. See Gordon, "The Relationship of Corporate Culture to Industry Sector and Performance."

9. For more information, see James Leahey and John Kotter, "British Airways," Harvard Business School Case No. 491-009.

10. For more on the ConAgra story, see Kotter, *A Force for Change,* chap. 10.

11. See Harvard Business School cases No. 381-174 (Aguilar), and No. 385-315 (Hamermesh), and GE's 1989 Annual Report.

12. To be discussed more fully in Chapter 9.

13. To be discussed more fully in Chapter 10.

14. For more on SAS, see Jan Carlzon, *Moments of Truth* (Cambridge, Mass.: Ballinger, 1987).

15. For more information on Gerstner and TRS, see Kotter, *A Force for Change,* chap. 3.

16. See Leonard Schlesinger and Todd Jick, "Xerox Corporation: Leadership Through Quality—Xerox in the 1980s," Harvard Business School Case No. 485-156.

17. Schein has noted something similar, especially regarding what we have called "unconventional insiders" (he calls them "hybrids").

18. Sarah Bartlett, "Bankers Trust Could Beat the Street at Its Own Game," *Business Week,* 4 April 1988, p. 87.

19. Ibid., p. 88.

20. See John P. Kotter, *The General Managers* (New York: Free Press, 1982); and *Power and Influence,* (New York: Free Press, 1985).

21. See Kotter, *The General Managers,* chap. 3; *Power and Influence,* chap. 4.

22. See *The Leadership Factor,* chapters 4, 5, and 6.

23. This is especially true for people who "grew up" in firms like those discussed in Chapter 6—firms that need cultural change.

8. LEADERS IN ACTION

1. The information on which this chapter is based comes from research conducted between 1987 and 1991. See Chapter 7, n. 4.

2. The literature on cultural change often states (or implies) that a major crisis is needed *before* organizations will appoint a strong leader to effect change. That is not what we have found.

3. A number of others have made a similar observation. See Schein, *Organizational Culture and Leadership,* Chapter 11.

4. For more on this process, see Kotter, *A Force for Change*, chap. 3.

5. For more on the process of communicating vision, see ibid., chap. 4.

6. For more on the process of motivation as used by leaders, see ibid., chap. 5.

7. As Michael Beer, Russell Eisenstat, and Bert Spector also report, managers in successful change efforts focus more on behavior than on values/ beliefs. See *The Critical Path* (Boston: Harvard Business School Press, 1990).

8. David Nadler and Michael Tushman have called this the "many-bullets" approach. See their "Organizational Frame Bending: Principles for Managing Reorientation," *Academy of Management Executive* 3 no. 3 (1989): 194–204.

9. Andrew Pettigrew, among others, has made the point that if cultural change does not reach the value level, the new culture will remain fragile and vulnerable, especially when the strong leader promoting change eventually retires. See his "Is Corporate Culture Manageable?" (Keynote Address at the Annual Strategic Management Society Conference, *Culture and Competitive Strategies*, Singapore, 13–16 October 1986).

10. Information on First Chicago comes from published sources and interviews conducted by Kotter at First Chicago in August 1989.

11. Suzanne Andrews, "Barry Sullivan's Chicago Crusade," *Institutional Investor*, July 1989, p. 61.

12. Others have drawn similar conclusions. See, for example, Rosabeth Kanter, Barry Stein, and Todd Jick, *The Challenge of Change* (New York: Free Press, 1992.)

13. Jick's discussion of the various roles people must successfully play is interesting in this regard. See Harvard Business School Note, "Implementing Change," No. 491-114.

9. THE CASE OF ICI

1. This chapter was prepared with the assistance of James Leahey, who drew heavily on previous work done by Andrew Pettigrew.

2. William J. Reader, *Imperial Chemical Industries: A History* (New York: Oxford University Press, 1975), vol. 2, p. 7.

3. Carol Kennedy, *ICI: The Company That Changed Our Lives* (London: Hutchinson, 1986), p. 140.

4. Andrew M. Pettigrew, *The Awakening Giant: Continuity and Change in Imperial Chemical Industries* (New York: Basil Blackwell, 1985), p. 82.

5. Geoffrey Foster, "The Legacy of Harvey-Jones," *Management Today*, January 1987, p. 36.
6. Pettigrew, *The Awakening Giant*, p. 388.
7. Ibid.
8. Ibid., p. 82.
9. Ibid., p. 376.
10. Ibid., p. 402.
11. Ibid., p. 409.
12. Ibid., p. 376.
13. Andrew Pettigrew, interview with Jim Leahey, Coventry, England, 1 August 1989.
14. Pettigrew, *The Awakening Giant*, p. 376.
15. Harvey-Jones, correspondence with Jim Leahey, 17 October 1989.
16. Sir John Harvey-Jones, *Making It Happen: Reflections on Leadership* (London: William Collins Sons & Company, 1988), p. 47.
17. Interview with Jim Leahey, 2 August 1989.
18. Edgar Vincent, interview with Jim Leahey, London, England, 28 July 1989.
19. Harvey-Jones, pp. 50 and 102.
20. Ibid., p. 194.
21. Foster, "The Legacy of Harvey-Jones," p. 41.
22. Vincent, interview.
23. Stephanie Cooke and John Tarpey, "Behind the Stunning Comeback at Britain's ICI/John Harvey-Jones: ICI's Jolly Captain," *Business Week* (Industrial/Technology Edition), 3 June 1985, p. 62.
24. Vincent, interview.
25. Interview with Jim Leahey, 2 August 1989.
26. Jonathan Hunt, "The Final Act of a Commanding Performance," *Chief Executive*, September 1986, p. 30.

10. THE CASE OF NISSAN

1. This chapter was prepared with the assistance of Nancy Rothbard.
2. Most of the information on Nissan comes from extensive interviews with Nissan managers conducted by Kotter in August 1990.
3. Company document.
4. Based on interviews conducted in Tokyo by Kotter.
5. The NTC, located in Atsugi (about two hours from Tokyo by car), is the center for design and technology at Nissan. Most of Nissan's R&D activity in Japan takes place at the NTC.
6. This quotation and all the others in this chapter are from interviews conducted by Kotter in August 1990.

7. Nissan offered to pay the interest rate on the loan the dealer took out to finance the remodeling. In other words, the dealer got a "free" loan.

8. Designers usually made at least two different clay models of a car to be submitted for final approval by the president. There had been occasions when the president liked one model and the chairman liked another. Designers would have to compromise and combine disparate parts of two models.

9. Some indicators are not as positive. Cash flow at Nissan, for example, grew increasingly negative during this period.

11. ON THE ROLE OF TOP MANAGEMENT

1. Wilkins has reported cases that show how fragile a good culture can be if top managers do not pay attention to it and don't do what is needed to preserve it. See his *Developing Corporate Character*.

BIBLIOGRAPHY

Aguilar, Frank J. "General Electric: Strategic Position, 1981," Harvard Business School Case No. 381-174, 1981.

Andrews, Suzanne. "Barry Sullivan's Chicago Crusade." *Institutional Investor*, July 1989, pp. 56–66.

Bartlett, Sarah. "Bankers Trust Could Beat the Street at Its Own Game." *Business Week*, 4 April 1988, pp. 86–88.

Beckhard, Richard. *Organization Development*. Reading, Mass.: Addison-Wesley, 1969.

Beer, Michael. *Organization Change and Development*. Glenview, Ill: Scott Foresman, 1980.

———, Russell Eisenstat, and Bert Spector. *The Critical Path*. Boston: Harvard Business School Press, 1990.

Benedict, Ruth. *Patterns of Culture*. Boston: Houghton Mifflin, 1934.

Beyer, Margaret H. *The Role of Corporate Cultures in the Management of High-Performing Banks*. University of Delaware, 1988.

Boas, Franz. "The Central Eskimo." Bureau of Ethnology Annual Report No. 6, pp. 399–664. Washington, D.C.: Smithsonian Institution, 1884.

Boyatzis, Richard E. *The Competent Manager*. New York: John Wiley & Sons, 1982.

Burns, Thomas, and G. M. Stalker. *The Management of Innovation*. London: Tavistock, 1961.

Carlzon, Jan. *Moments of Truth*. Cambridge, Mass.: Ballinger, 1987.

Chemical Industry Association. "Basic International Chemical Industry Statistics 1963–1986." 1987. Chart 6.

Cleveland, Harold van B., and Thomas F. Huertas. *Citibank 1812–1970*. Cambridge: Harvard University Press, 1985.

Cooke, Stephanie, and John Tarpey. "Behind the Stunning Comeback at Britain's ICI/John Harvey-Jones: ICI's Jolly Captain." *Business Week* (Industrial/Technology Edition), 3 June 1985, pp. 62–63.

Davis, Stanley M. *Managing Corporate Culture*. Cambridge, Mass.: Ballinger, 1984.

Deal, Terry E., and Allan A. Kennedy. *Corporate Cultures*. Reading, Mass.: Addison-Wesley, 1982.

Denison, Daniel. *Corporate Culture and Organizational Effectiveness*. New York: John Wiley & Sons, 1990.

Dessauer, John H. *My Years with Xerox*. Garden City, N.Y.: Doubleday, 1971.

Donaldson, Gordon, and Jay Lorsch. *Decision Making at the Top*. New York: Basic Books, 1983.

Drucker, Peter. *Management: Tasks, Responsibilities, Practices*. New York: Harper & Row, 1974.

Fitzgerald, Thomas. "Can Change in Organizational Culture Really Be Managed?" *Organizational Dynamics* 17, no. 2 (Autumn 1988): 4.

Foster, Geoffrey. "The Legacy of Harvey-Jones." *Management Today*, January 1987, pp. 34–41, 86–88.

Gordon, George G. "The Relationship of Corporate Culture to Industry Sector and Corporate Performance." In Kilmann, Saxton, and Serpa, eds. *Gaining Control of the Corporate Culture*, pp. 103–125.

Hamermesh, Richard G. "General Electric Co., 1984," Harvard Business School Case No. 385-315, 1985.

Harvey-Jones, Sir John. *Making it Happen: Reflections on Leadership*. London: William Collins Sons & Company, 1988.

Hofstede, Geert. *Culture's Consequences*. Beverly Hills, Calif.: Sage, 1980.

Homans, George. *The Human Group*. New York: Harcourt, Brace & World, 1950.

Hunt, Jonathan. "The Final Act of a Commanding Performance." *Chief Executive*, September 1986, pp. 30–31.

Hutchison, Robert. *Off the Books*. New York: William Morrow, 1986.

Jacobson, Gary, and John Hillkirk. *Xerox: American Samurai*. New York: Macmillan, 1986.

Jick, Todd. "The Challenge of Change," Harvard Business School Note No. 490-016, 1989.

———. "Implementing Change," Harvard Business School Note No. 491-114, 1991.

Kanter, Rosabeth M. *The Change Masters*. New York: Simon & Schuster, 1983.

———, Barry Stein, and Todd Jick. *The Challenge of Change*. New York: Free Press, 1992.

Katz, Donald R. *The Big Store*. New York: Viking Penguin, 1987.

Keller, Maryann. *Rude Awakening*. New York: William Morrow, 1989.

Kennedy, Carol. *ICI: The Company That Changed Our Lives*. London: Hutchinson, 1986.

Kilmann, Ralph H., M. J. Saxton, and Roy Serpa, eds. *Gaining Control of the Corporate Culture*. San Francisco: Jossey-Bass, 1986.

Kotter, John P. *A Force for Change: How Leadership Differs from Management*. New York: Free Press, 1990.

———. *The General Managers*. New York: Free Press, 1982.

———. *The Leadership Factor*. New York: Free Press, 1988.

———. *Power and Influence*. New York: Free Press, 1985.

———, Leonard Schlesinger, and Vijay Sathe. *Organization: Text, Cases, and Readings on the Management of Organization Design and Change*. 2d ed. Homewood, Ill.: Richard D. Irwin, 1986.

Lawrence, Paul, and Jay Lorsch. *Organization and Environment*. Boston: Harvard Business School Press, 1967.

Leahey, James, and John Kotter. "Changing the Culture at British Airways," Harvard Business School Case No. 491-009, 1990.

Likert, Rensis. *The Human Organization*. New York: McGraw-Hill, 1967.

Louis, Meryl. "Sourcing Workplace Cultures: Why, When, and How." In Kilmann, Saxton, and Serpa, eds., *Gaining Control of the Corporate Culture*, 126–136.

Malinowski, Bronislaw. *Argonauts of the Western Pacific: An Account of Native Enterprise and Adventure in the Archipelagoes of Melanesian New Guinea*. London: George Routledge & Sons, 1922.

March, James G., ed. *Handbook of Organizations*. Chicago: Rand McNally, 1965.

Nadler, David, and Michael Tushman. "Organizational Frame Bending: Principles for Managing Reorientation." *Academy of Management Executive* 3, no. 3 (1989): 194–204.

Ouchi, William. *Theory Z*. Reading, Mass.: Addison-Wesley, 1981.

Pascale, Richard T., and Anthony G. Athos. *The Art of Japanese Management*. New York: Simon & Schuster, 1981.

Peters, Tom, and Nancy Austin. *A Passion for Excellence: The Leadership Difference.* New York: Random House, 1985.

——, and R. H. Waterman. *In Search of Excellence.* New York: Harper & Row, 1982.

Pettigrew, Andrew M. *The Awakening Giant: Continuity and Change in Imperial Chemical Industries.* New York: Basil Blackwell, 1985.

——. "Conclusion: Organizational Climate and Culture: Two Constructs in Search of a Role." In Schneider, ed., *Organizational Climate and Culture,* pp. 413–433.

——. "On Studying Organizational Culture." *Administrative Science Quarterly* 24 (1979): 570–581.

——. "Is Corporate Culture Manageable?" Keynote Address at the Annual Strategic Management Society Conference, *Culture and Competitive Strategies.* Singapore, 13–16 October 1986.

Radcliffe-Brown, A. R. "The Mother's Brother in South Africa." *South African Journal of Science* 21 (1924): 542–555.

Reader, William J. *Imperial Chemical Industries: A History.* Vol. II. New York: Oxford University Press, 1975.

Roethlisberger, Fritz J., and William J. Dickson. *Management and the Worker: An Account of a Research Program Conducted by the Western Electric Company, Hawthorne Works, Chicago.* Cambridge: Harvard University Press, 1939.

Rousseau, Denise. "Assessing Organizational Culture: The Case for Multiple Methods." In Schneider, ed., *Organizational Climate and Culture,* pp. 153–192.

Sathe, Vijay. *Culture and Related Corporate Realities.* Homewood, Ill.: Richard D. Irwin, 1985.

Schein, Edgar H. *Organizational Culture and Leadership.* San Francisco: Jossey-Bass, 1985.

——. "Organizational Socialization and Profession of Management." *Industrial Management Review* 9 (1968): 1–15.

Schlesinger, Leonard, and Todd Jick. "Xerox Corporation: Leadership through quality—Xerox in the 1980s," Harvard Business School Case No. 485-156, 1985.

Schneider, Benjamin ed. *Organizational Climate and Culture.* San Francisco: Jossey-Bass, 1990.

Selznick, Philip. *Leadership in Administration.* New York: Harper & Row, 1957.

Siehl, Caren, and Joanne Martin. "Culture: A Key To Financial Performance?" In Schneider, ed., *Organizational Climate and Culture,* pp. 241–281.

Smith, Douglas K., and Robert C. Alexander. *Fumbling the Future.* New York: William Morrow, 1988.

Tichy, Noel M., and Mary Anne Devanna. *The Transformational Leader*. New York: John Wiley & Sons, 1986.

Tylor, Edward B. *Primitive Culture: Researches into the Development of Mythology, Philosophy, Religion, Art, and Custom*. 2 vols. New York: Henry Holt, 1887.

Uttal, Bro. "The Corporate Culture Vultures," *Fortune*, 17 October 1983, pp. 66–72.

Van Manenn, John. "People Processing: Strategies of Organizational Socialization." In Sathe, Vijay, *Culture and Related Corporate Realities*, pp. 223–243.

Wilkins, Alan L. *Developing Corporate Character*. San Francisco: Jossey-Bass, 1989.

———, and Kerry J. Patterson. "You Can't Get There from Here: What Will Make Cultural Change Projects Fail." In Kilmann, Saxton, and Serpa, eds., *Gaining Control of the Corporate Culture*, pp. 262–291.

Wright, J. P. *On a Clear Day You Can See General Motors*. Grosse Pointe, Mich.: Wright Enterprises. 1979.

INDEX